"During our twenties, we are truly just trying to figure everything out, and we cast wide nets, sometimes hoping for something to stick. Or we cast nets hoping for the surprise of something new because even with everything planned out, we still aren't sure, and we're young. Things can change if we want them to."

The twenties are such an interesting decade. It is a time when we grow beyond our adolescence, beyond friends, beyond a career, beyond the flings, and into learning who we are meant to be. It is a decade that proves to be a glorious ride. Faithfully, we grow into who God intends.

A GARDEN IN BLOOM:

Faith that grows in your twenties

Ayomide Adebayo

A Garden In Bloom
Copyright © 2024 Ayomide Adebayo

ISBN 979-8-9903093-0-2 - Paperback
ISBN 979-8-9903093-1-9 - Ebook

Cover Design by Charlei H.

First U.S. Edition
Printed in the United States of America

1 Corinthians 3:6-9

"I planted. Apollos watered. But God gave the increase. **7** So then neither he who plants is anything, nor he who waters, but God who gives the increase. **8** Now he who plants and he who waters are the same, but each will receive his own reward according to his own labor.**9** For we are God's fellow workers. You are God's farming, God's building."

In dedication to Oyinkansola Oshundun-Ogundiran, for watering me and shining light when you did, thank you for helping my garden bloom.

Introduction

I started writing in 2013 during the Christmas season. I was struggling to process the death of my aunt. I didn't know yet that God was about to fill me up to grow and have a story to tell. I started writing a book about death and grief. However, as I allowed life to move ahead and God to mold and heal me, I realized that He would show me how to live.

I remember when I turned 20. I wore this white skirt and pink peplum tank and had the cutest weave. The weave only lasted two weeks because it hurt so terribly. I was extra cute for two weeks. I remember this birthday because I had the time of my life spending it in New York with a dear friend. I remember that same summer, I fell for someone and learned to live without someone else. I cannot say that I remember each significant moment in my twenties, but I remember the ones that shaped, crafted, and made me. I'm sure we have those moments whether we want them or not. I can pinpoint the times that I practically withered away into nothing and the many times and the many people that caused me to bloom beautifully into the fullness of myself. Indeed, being in your twenties is a story-filled decade for every individual.

We should recognize that when a flower blooms, it does not just go from seed to flower, but rather the success of the plant, and many things in this life, lies not only in the environment that it is in but also in the faith to bloom. For me, it was faith in God. The seed for this book was planted when I was 19. Of course, at that moment, I did not know it then, but ten years later, birthed out of tears, frustration, light, love, forgiveness, a whole lot of clarity, and a whole lot more freedom and discipline, I was able to bring this into fruition. Just as it has often been said, " A rose from concrete," I bloomed. So I want to share my garden with you all, if you'll let me. I want to show what it looks like and feels like to grow in many forms and come out beautiful. My twenties were full of weeds and flowers; some areas needed replanting and some straight-up uprooting. Some needed more watering than others. But with anything in the garden, you must be patient and willing to get dirty.

If you have already made it to the bottom of this introduction, know that for that alone, I am eternally grateful. Around the age of 24, I remember telling a friend that I wanted to write a book, and she quickly said: " Don't tell me when you want it to be done because you will put pressure on yourself; just write, and when it's done I'll read it." Well, my friends, it's here. I titled the book ' A Garden in Bloom' because I am often reminded that my life began with the greatest Gardener. The world first took place in a garden, and it was there that God revealed himself to Adam and Eve.

It was often in times of quiet and reflection that God revealed himself to me. So come along with me as we bloom and grow, in hopefully more ways than one. I believe I am only a vessel for what God wants to use this book for. As you read and relate, I pray you understand that in your blooming moments, because you will have them, and in your uprooting, because you will have those too, they all come together moment by moment and create A Garden in Bloom.

A flower starts as a seed, tiny and unknown.
What grows from within has the ability to stand tall and beautiful.
It took me a while to understand that even in its nourishment, a
flower must lose a few leaves to **bloom.**

Part 1: The Seed

"For I know the thoughts that I think toward you," says Yahweh, "thoughts of peace, and not of evil, to give you hope and a future."

- Jeremiah 29:11

Chapter One

M y pastor once said during a sermon, "Something is wrong when our lives make sense to unbelievers," that stuck with me. His statement stuck with me because, at that moment, I had to recognize that I had spent a lot of time trying to be easy and relatable and trying to make sense of everything so that others could understand me. I was okay being Switzerland, trying not to rock the boat in any particular direction so everyone would feel safe and validated. However, I look back and see now more than ever that it wasn't just that I wanted to be a neutral party in life, but I was often afraid of not being understood, and many times, I didn't even understand myself. I was scared to grow.

Things have changed now. I am no longer afraid to be misunderstood because I do not desire to be understood. I desire for people to understand how I moved out of my fears. I desire for folks to know that in my hiding and silence, I was being sought after by the Holy Spirit. As He filled my heart and mind to be sure of myself and know who I am, I was filled with the courage and joy that would draw others to come to know Him. Learning to live a life where the Holy Spirit was living in me did not come naturally. Understanding we are born with a sinful nature, we can operate in resistance. I didn't go to a service one day and " catch the Holy Ghost." God was always present in my life; I just had to acknowledge Him. I was resistant, but mercy kept me and has kept me longer than resistance ever would. Here I was at 18, moving to a new city on my own. I was anything but aware, yet He kept me.

It was August 12th, 2012, and while I am sure all new college freshmen were giddy and excited to be packing and leaving their homes and start their journey as college students, I had my mind set on the real prize: one more free meal at IHOP before the hunger of a college student began. I went ahead and ordered a fully loaded omelet with pancakes and enjoyed the moment I was having with my family. In the next few hours, I would head off to the best HBCU in the nation, The Black Harvard, The Mecca, the Illustrious Howard University. That's right, folks. I was starting as a freshman accounting major in the amazing business school that I would have to say goodbye to in a year, but let's not get ahead of ourselves; after all, it was move-in day. I was excited, nervous, scared, all normal, and rightfully so. But most of all, I was unprepared. I did not know it on the first day or the next day, but in the coming weeks, I would quickly learn that I was unprepared for my college journey.

Let's take a second to think about it: are any of us ready to be on our own and start living a little on our own? Individual circumstances and upbringings play a role in development. However, in the big picture, nobody is ever ready to do anything on their own. It's a change. You can't prepare for it, but it must happen anyway. Perhaps I could say that I was academically ready since I did get into the university. I could also infer that growing up as the firstborn, I had the maturity and mental discipline to be on my own. Physically, I hadn't changed, and I wouldn't let the freshman fifteen change me too much. However, I'm talking about spirituality. Was I spiritually ready for what I was going to be exposed to? It would take me a while to catch up to where life was about to take me. With my lack of understanding and defenses low, there was no better time and place than college. Weeds that were planted easily would show themselves later as I matriculated in school, but it would be ok, and I would be ok.

Nonetheless, I was going to enjoy my time at Howard; your girl was out of the house! Away and on her own to do anything she wanted, and yet I was not a reckless person. In college, you may have your first bits of alcohol and find yourself at a couple of parties. For me, that scene got old very quickly. Aside from the occasional functions and events, I spent much of my time in my room eating Papa John's (shoutout rewards for the many free pizzas) and binging on the whole series of *Girlfriends*. I spent time exploring DC before it became brunch central, becoming an expert on the metro, getting woken up because someone had to borrow leggings for an event, and just going through each other's closets. I spent my free moments making noodles with my contraband microwave and creating memories from enduring the torrential downpour of rain at my first official Homecoming, where Drake surprised us all. You hear some horror stories of roommates and suitemates, but I genuinely had the most fantastic roommate 10/10 shoutout to Brooklyn! I lived on the best floor in the Quad. I had so much fun living the dorm life and met the most amazing people from all walks of life. I enjoyed the mundane moments. I loved it. I was sleeping most of my days, eating a lot at the café, having plenty of girl nights, failing a math course, and figuring it all out. This was the gist of my first semester, and I will say God's hand was on me still. For every party I attended, I would still be in church the following morning, barely able to keep my eyes open, but I was in the building. I can say from experience that many of us are in the building, and that doesn't mean anything about our lives, but God's mercy.

In all the adjusting, learning, and fun that was happening, I quickly learned that life was about balance. Well, I tipped the scale too far. I experienced my bit of freedom and went from the top 10 of my class in high school to academic probation in college, talk about range. I did not realize it back then, but I lacked discipline and self-control, even though I knew they were necessary.

The Bible talks of self-control as one of the Fruit of the Spirit listed in Gal 5:22-23 by which, as believers, we should live our lives bearing the fruit. Self-control is a piece of the fruit that many of us tend to lack. We may often fixate on the now and the necessity of wanting something now that we miss the need to wait. We also need more patience, which is another fruit. We enjoy the instant gratifications of life, and sometimes, it may come at a fault. Without such things, we are left vulnerable, easily swayed, and without restraint. We are left to the will of the world, our thoughts, and our emotions. For the wrong person and wrong thing, it could be a spiral waiting to happen.

I was that wrong person again with no fruit because, suddenly, everything was spiraling right in front of me. I sat with my eyes frozen on the screen. I had never been great at math, but how did I fail an entire class? I struggled through lessons, exams, and so many formulas, but to fail me felt a bit much on the professor's part. However, I had to take responsibility. My parents had just scrambled to get $16,000 for my first semester, and I completely blew it out of the universe. I was supposed to find a way to get financial aid for the following semester through a scholarship or something, and here I was, racking up debt and wasting money at that. A lot of people would like to say, "Oh no, don't worry about it, it's just your first semester, and you are adjusting to college. You will do better next semester." Although I believed them, I knew I was capable of so much more than what was being shown on screen. I knew I did not put in the studying time, office hours, or make the connections to ace the course, and now I had to pay, literally, to retake it the following fall semester. I had to buckle down and knew I would get it right. The best thing a person can do is learn to take responsibility early.

I didn't let the situation hinder me for too long because I knew what needed to be done next semester. One semester down, seven more to go. I was in college, a new church, renewing my faith in the Lord and enjoying the community it brought along. I allowed myself to enter the spring semester; this time, it was me, my books, one random self-defense class that scared me to pieces, and whatever Rom-Com I could watch that weekend. DC in the spring was an absolute vibe, but seeing that 3.5 and getting off of academic probation was even better. Like I said earlier, I know what I am capable of. I just need to be honest with myself and apply self-control to be successful. I was not going to spiral.

So, the spring semester was looking up, and I was on a good path. It was spring break, and while many of my friends went to Panama City for spring break, I went to Dallas, Texas, to spend time with my aunt. I feel like I partially didn't get the college spring break on the beach memo, but also, knowing me, I would not have had that much of a time, so I was better off in Texas with my favorite person. For as long as I can remember, I have spent summers, winters, and random moments of celebration with my aunt, so being with her during spring break was going to be our usual good time.

When I sit at this moment and think about it, my spring break in Texas was our last time together in her home, our last shopping spree where she got me whatever I wanted. I remember this denim vest with a chiffon bottom piece she bought me. It's not my style now, but I could not take it off that semester. It was our last time binging Cartoon Network together, and I never knew it, so I treated life casually because what else could be done? She didn't know it either. You never know when it will be your last time seeing anybody in life, whether dead or alive. Life happens, so you stop, recalibrate, keep going, and learn to adjust. It may be as final as life and death, or someone moves away, or a new job appears. Think of how many people we stop seeing.

From the week of spring break up until the fall season, time flew at a speed I didn't recognize, yet it was slow enough for me to remember unique details. You see, in summary, April 1st was the day that my aunt was diagnosed with cancer. May was the month that I thought I found love. In June, I began interning at a hospital (which had nothing to do with my career path). July and August were spent nursing my aunt back to health with my little cousins nearby. September, my mother lost her job, I dropped out of college, and my aunt was gone forever.

In small doses, these are all just seeds that life hands us, and we figure out what to do as time goes along. They grow as a part of our story. However, when you think about it, nobody should go through so much change in varying areas without a solid force nearby. In the spring and summer of 2013, life was coming at me quickly, and I was starting to do well academically. I had someone who was remotely into me. I was cute and happy to be here. By the time it was fall and winter that same year, I wanted to run and hide. I took the seeds that life handed me and buried them because, in my broken mind, how could life bear any fruit with the season I was in? My faith did not prepare me for any of this, yet God showed himself to be an anchor.

Chapter Two

A twenty-minute walk, one bus, a shuttle, one train, two metro stops, and 3 hours later, I arrived on campus for my 8 am biology lab. This was my new reality as a commuter from Baltimore to Washington, DC, almost every day for the entire third semester. The journey served as a great distraction at times. The days of no commuting were because of the blessing of friendship when I would stay with a friend for the night to keep a sense of normalcy from everything else happening at home. I didn't have the luxury of staying on campus that year. It was expensive. I had other priorities. I didn't have the luxury of seeing all my friends the same way, hanging out just because, or going to one event or another. There was no Drake or Howard Homecoming period for me.

I also couldn't drive yet, so I depended on all forms of public transportation. It wasn't all too bad, as I had a friend living with me, and we would commute some days together, but hers was much shorter. The only consistent factor to my fall semester from the last fall semester was that SPOILER ALERT: I did not pass the math course again. However, I would like to say that with the cards I was dealt with the last four months, the fact that I showed up and passed anything at all was by the grace of God. I almost failed three classes, but tears and persuasion brought me to a C. I wouldn't be back after this semester anyway, so I had nothing to lose. Even the little faith I thought I had was floating through rocky soil.

Hebrews chapter eleven, verse one, tells us that "faith is the assurance of things hoped for, proof of things not seen." To have evidence of things not seen is an oxymoron; to natural beings, invisible evidence does not align with the standard of what is considered evident. I guess it is just something for people to hold on to, a way to place one foot in front of the other even when you do not know the direction to take. The Bible says a lot of things, but how much do we acknowledge? How often do we apply it into action in our lives, not just on a poster or tattoo or a verse sitting on a profile to show we have a sense of moral judgment?

I suppose faith is more than "hope." Some may argue it to be the same, like when a young child waits for Santa to come down the chimney. So, let's examine faith together. Specifically, let's talk about faith in a time of grief. When somebody you care for gets sick, you say a prayer, and when it is answered, life goes on because there is faith. With faith, we can trust that God has healed. When you watch someone you love get sick and then die, you continue to pray and hope and pray and hope for a miracle. Yet the curse of knowledge has made you realize the survival rate is zero percent, but you still keep on praying. That is still faith, too, right? Has the faith changed from faith to heal to faith to restore from grief? Is it still faith if you shift in what you had faith in?

A Garden in Bloom

My aunt is gone. She did not go to Paris, Brazil, or London, although she has been there. She didn't buy some new shoes for her "Vince Camuto" collection. She wasn't playing Hide and Seek, even though she was very good at that, herself and my mother. She died. My heart is heavy, shattered, as I write. I speak to her daughter and watch her grow into herself. I think to myself, you should be doing this. I am her cousin, and I give her advice as a cousin. I'll fill in whatever she cannot get through you, all the little things left over after you have perfectly brought her up to become a young woman. All the little things she may think you don't need to know and will tell me instead because I am younger and cooler. It should be you guiding her through these moments yourself, but here, my mother is taking on that new role. Here I am with an even heavier role than just a big cousin, and it feels strange. We don't even exist in the same state, yet when everyone close by seems to have left, we must learn how to be present from afar, love from afar, and show up from afar. I can imagine what jokes you would make as she gave you drama in her teenage years. Your affluent nature would impress on her the finer things in life while balancing its simplicity, just as you did for me.

You would straighten the path when she made a stain with her lipstick or had on too much eye shadow. When she had to go to cheerleading practice, start her period, or prepare for prom and then college, you would be there. No matter the journey, you would have a joke, and it would end with a smile, bringing us back at ease. You would be there for your son's first girlfriend and report back to my mom all the problems you had with the girl while sucking your teeth. You would show up to show your girls dressed to the nines for their graduations and weddings. You were supposed to be there with us for all of life. No moment was too small, and no moment was to be cut short. You were supposed to be there for me.

Death sent us mail, but I guess you can say we threw it in the trash. I mean, why would I want to open such a letter? We had been sent the notifications all year, but we said nope, our faith is strong. We do not need to open the letter. Death sent some more letters, emails, texts, everything you can think to prepare us, but we were not having it. My mother lost her job on a Monday. I decided to drop out of university on Wednesday (unbeknownst to my family yet) because of financial circumstances. Death knocked this time on Thursday, as an alleged bomb alert went off near the metro of my workplace; surprisingly, this was not even big local news even though they sent us home early. I guess it would seem that I was having quite an eventful week. The odds were indeed not in my favor, but I continued to show up for life. Through it all, I continued to smile. I remember sitting in front of the financial aid building, telling a friend that week, "What else could go wrong?" I guess it is true when they say that words have power. Finally, death, so unkind, barged in early Friday morning, took my aunt, and left. I suppose we can say that the week was intense. We can say that God showed all the signs, and I should have been prepared for this moment, that it was bound to happen, and that He would cover me through. We can say that everyone is going to die someday, and she is in a better place; she has transcended to glory. However, who prepares for death?

On Friday, September 13th, 2013, my world came crumbling down. I can vividly remember that day. Sometimes, it's too vivid a memory that I believe I am delusional. We always hear "Friday the 13th" as a day of bad luck, but who really believes in that stuff? This already sounds like a joke, "My aunt passed away on Friday the 13th," bizarre huh? Well, that is exactly what had happened. To even add to the strange irony of it all, she was diagnosed with cancer on April 1, 2013, that's right, April Fools Day.

Despite the previous events of the week, after work, my Thursday continued as usual. My friend decided to stay over at her school from Thursday to Saturday because of a Caribbean event that was going to happen. The plan was to meet her that Friday to go out, but I told her I was not yet sure I would be attending because I was not in the mood but wanted to be there. I wanted a release from the tension that was building up. My mood had been mellow throughout the week; mellow moods are not my best asset. I should have realized that something bad was going to happen. I should have realized a lot of things. Taking the blame for a lot of situations that "I do not have control over" is a delivered pastime. Yet, I should have noticed a shift. I would like to believe there is a universal shift when a significant life event happens concerning somebody. God is maybe saying, "Prepare for turbulence; we're headed into a quick storm." However, this storm was not short. I had a math exam the next day, so taking advantage of an empty room, I spent the remainder of the night studying because I could not afford to fail again. College was too expensive. I did not feel like taking the test because math and I were still not friends, but I did not know I would miss the exam under such circumstances. I said my prayers. I went to sleep.

Around 5:30, if not earlier in the morning, I started hearing noises. I did not look at my phone, so I figured it was just my siblings getting ready for school, even though the noise did not sound like preparing for school. But the screaming was gut-wrenching. My mom threw open the door, "Your auntie is dead!" she screamed. I thought I was having a nightmare; it had to be a joke. This could not be happening. Me? My auntie? Dead? It could not be possible. Things like death did not occur in my family. I had never experienced it. Death was something I heard about from afar, on television, and in books, but not in my actual life, with my loved ones.

My grandparents were still alive. I thought the Bible said that a parent should not have to bury their child. She even said to my mother, " sister, I will not die; this will not be unto death; I will fight it." No, this could not be happening. My world was spinning. This began to feel like an awful movie, with no commercial break or intermission, just one long Lifetime drama. This must be some storm God was bringing me through because I had yet to see the light in what just turned pitch black. I had never heard of such a thing since I was alive, but now it was happening, and the inevitable had come to pass. I did not know when the tears started pouring, but I fell to the floor, crying and crying. It was not an ordinary cry, the cry of agony, a wail that could not be understood.

My mother paced back and forth on the phone, screaming through the hallway. I could not figure out whom she was talking to. At one point, she spoke to those in Dallas, and at another point, probably her best friend. Left and right, she came and went, screaming through the hallway, talking, quiet, and screaming again. Confusion swept through the house. Suddenly, the phones rang, bringing life to the horrible truth. My sisters came to join me, awoken; they too, began to cry. They did not cry in agony like my mother and I cried. I was surprised they cried at all.

I do not even remember when I found my brother in the corner of his room crying, but it broke my heart. Did he truly understand the magnitude of the situation right now? It hurt that the relationship I was able to have with my auntie they never had, and they would never be able to have. They mourned over a loss that could not compare to the loss I felt. They knew she was no longer here, but that was different for me. If she was no longer here I too was in a way no longer here, and they still were. She was a part of me. She was a part of me that, for many years, I could not express because she had children, and their grief was even heavier. I had to put mine on hold. I had to be present.

My siblings were not staying home with all that was going on. We did not want them to witness the tragedy that was our life at the moment, let them stay behind the scenes if they could. I quickly called my aunt's cell phone, no response. I called a second and a third time, refusing to believe the nightmare unraveling in the early morning. I called my cousins, ready to trample them with questions, but they did not answer. Lucky for me, because they did not even know yet. They went to school and would be told when they got back. The world was already catching the news. My friend! She had to be notified; after all, she had grown to know Auntie very well. I wish everybody had known her when she was healthy; that was my auntie. She answered the phone, and I could tell I had woken her up.

"Sis, wake up, please," my voice was cracking.

"Ayomide, what's wrong?" She asked.

"Auntie..." I could not say it. I could not get the words out of my mouth.

"What happened to Auntie?" I did not respond.

"Ayomide, what? What? What is it?" she urged on.

"She's dead. Auntie is dead. Mommy said she thinks you should come home or stay if you want to." I hung up the phone.

I figured by the way I heard my dad talking in the background that my friend had called him to confirm. The house was in complete chaos, and it was only 6 in the morning. The sun wasn't up yet. I don't think that the sun ever came up that day. My mom ran into my room a second time, "Call your uncle! Call him now!" she screamed. My uncle and auntie were close, or at least I thought they were. Life is just full of illusions and interpretations. He was born after her. Their birthdays were one day apart. When she came over the summer before her death, he was supposed to see her, but he never showed up. She was here for over a month. He said he would come and see her, but he did not. Did he not realize she was sick? She and I tried to figure out a way to meet him, but he did not answer our calls. His absence hurt and broke her to pieces.

On her last day in Maryland, she lay on the kitchen chair and cried out, "My brother has run from me; he did not come and see me because I have cancer; what have I done to him?" Imagine someone you love and would put your heart on the line for, as if DNA did not make you all close enough, to abandon you now and ignore you while you die. Well, the phone rang that morning, and my uncle answered. He had not answered for weeks, but he answered at this moment. After weeks of trying to get through to him, he answers the phone at around 5:30 am on a Friday! I wondered why he was not asleep. Maybe he was getting ready for work; after this news, he wouldn't be going to work anymore, that's for sure. My mother grabbed the phone. In such a short matter of time, she was becoming increasingly aggressive through despair.

There was yelling from my mom, a lot of yelling, and then she threw the phone back at me. I did not know what to do with it because I surely had nothing else to say, so I hung up, whether he was still on the phone or not. I would forgive him in time.

The doorbell rang, and a family friend of ours walked in; from that point on, it was a revolving door all day. She began to console my mother as she broke down. She didn't break down. Her life had just shattered into a trillion tiny glass pieces. Mine had too. She had lost a sister, someone she had grown up with since birth. My mother knew her more than everybody else: her friends, her husband, her other siblings, everybody except my grandparents who gave birth to her; they were on another level. She only had one sister, and now she was only one sister. However, I had lost somebody as well. I lost an aunt, a best friend, a second mother, a counselor, a bodyguard, and a piece of my heart. When I think about a hurt heart, this was probably where it grew from. Everybody recognized the husband and her kids; of course, they should be consoled rightly so, as they were the immediate family. Many people also remembered my mother and consoled her because she was her only sister. However, people forgot the rest of the family, the other siblings in Nigeria, and the other nieces and nephews. Many people forgot us. Many people forgot me.

They forgot that I was also hurting and that I loved her and still do love her more than anything in this world. They had forgotten our relationship from endless summers to endless winters to endless springs and falls. We spent so much time together. She showed up for me in every way she could. She was at my last graduation front and center, and it was me and her that went to Macy's with my mom afterward, side by side. She was to me indescribable, but with a smile, she could describe it all. When that smile was stilled on the morning of September, my life became a blank book. The pages that were once full of hopes and dreams and desires with the support of my aunt had now been torn away and burned into ashes, and now I was being forced to rewrite a new life that I never imagined. I never imagined life without her. Texas was our distance, and I flew there so frequently that it felt like no distance. Even as I got older, we would both still cry, separating when one of us had to go through TSA.

On her passing, I was told just to be strong; it is God's will. Circumstances had brought a whole new meaning to the word "life," and for a long time, I felt no reason to participate in it. I was never suicidal, just not an active participant. When I look back on September 2013 and the months to come, I don't know how I was able to function in any capacity. I was truly numb. I felt no reason to be a part of something so temporary that at any moment, you could become cold and hard like a stone, back to the dust where we were created. Experiencing loss does something to you that you are never prepared for. Whether you see it coming or not, if you are young or old, I believe it puts a strain on the heart and view of life, that only God himself can help restore.

It is funny, the situations of life. It is also funny how God answers prayers. When you look in the Bible and recall the story of the Israelites and how God saved the firstborn sons by telling the people of Israel to mark the doorpost with the Lamb's blood, and death will crossover, you cannot help but ask yourself, should I have done the same? Maybe a mark of blood around Auntie would have prevented her death, but it does not work that way. We had pastors on speed dial, and still. Constantly and constantly, questions will always be asked, but an answer will never come. The answer won't come because we continue to look on the surface rather than ask the Doer and Creator himself. This situation brought to light the true essence of faith. Will we still believe, trust, and love God when tragedy strikes? We are quick to thank Him and praise Him when everything is going well. When things are bad, we quickly mock Him and question His reasoning; we humans can be terrible people. We lack knowledge and blame it on the ignorance of the world around us. However, we forget that in the Bible, God talks to us, saying in 2 Corinthians 10:3 that although we are in the world, we are not of the world. I was full of anger during this time. And though I knew the Word, it was not in my heart to do anything for me at this time. I had no roots.

The day of her death was a different one for me. I had mixed emotions that day. I mourned like a child of the world because, at that moment, life had just left the world, and ignoring the fact that she was free from pain and suffering, I continued to mourn because, in the end, she was not with me. Is that not selfish? Ignoring the fact that she had gone to find peace and joy and rest in the heavenly arms of our Lord and Savior, it did not matter to me because I could no longer rest in her arms, and no longer could her children be touched by her gentle motherly hands, and no longer could there be a smile to be seen. At that moment when death had encompassed the house, and I needed the Lord more than ever, I could not reach Him. I could not reach Him because I did not want to be reached. I wanted an explanation. If death was going to come, at least explain to me why! I wailed in agony on my knees as the sun rose. Unseen was its brightness that autumn day when darkness had covered the house. The day had not started yet, and I already wanted it to end.

A Garden in Bloom

It was all still a blur, and it was not even 8 in the morning. The day seemed to be going so slow yet so fast. I don't know when she arrived, but another family friend of ours was in the house talking to my mother, and things were beginning to settle for a few minutes. I continued to call my aunt, but she did not answer the phone. My mom's best friend soon walked in also on the phone. I am sure she called the whole state of Maryland for mommy. How many people had entered the house? Would the phone ever stop ringing? Is this really happening right now? All I could do was sit. I must have cried my eyes out in the morning and was surely going crazy because, for some reason, my aunt wanted me to go to school. Seriously? Do you want me to take a 2-hour train ride and take an exam in the state I'm in? No. No, thank you, not happening. My siblings were shipped out of the house quickly. They did get ready for school, and my dad took them. They were unprepared for the bus. I wonder how they operated in school that day. I don't even remember them coming back home later that day; it's unbelievable the selective memory of the brain during trauma.

My friend finally made it home and then disappeared to go and cry in the bathroom. Time was moving at a rate I could not comprehend. The doorbell continued to ring, and people came in. They cried, my mom cried, I cried; it was just a huge tear fest. My dad did not cry, well, at least to my knowledge. He did not cry until the day that we buried her, and I am happy because if he had cried on the day she died, that is every member of the house in shambles. We all sat in the house, and people called through the phone, screaming in disbelief. It was still morning. This day was painfully long. My family tried to get me to eat but I was not having it. I couldn't fathom doing anything and wanted to be left alone. I did not eat that entire day, and my mother began to scream at me.

"Do you want me to start worrying about you also? I need you to eat and be strong, please! Do not let me begin to worry." Again, I was to be strong.

I guess crying so much can make you lose weight, but I was just not hungry, so I drank hot chocolate and retreated to my bedroom. Myself, my friend staying with me at the time, and another friend of mine stayed in my room. One of my aunts felt that I did not need to be downstairs with all the crying and that they would take care of my mom, who also had not eaten anything. We did not speak or watch the television; we just sat there. My friend tried to have a conversation with me, but I did not have anything to say.

It was just the beginning of the afternoon when I heard the garage door open and went downstairs to see that it was Papa. Papa was who we called our longtime family pastor and friend. If I could not stay downstairs, I still felt the right to know who was in my house, so I checked the doors. I was so happy to see Papa and Mama, who had come straight from their trip, that I ran straight to hug them and began to cry. Papa just smiled and said, "It is well". I never understood that statement of his, and in the beginning, it just bothered me that such a person could exist, always joyful, never stressed. That was the power of God. This was something I would come to understand later. Well, that is how he entered the house that

21

day. I almost wanted him to say something else besides that statement. I was ready to go off, but I kept quiet. I wasn't an animal. I did have respect. Papa met my mom upstairs and spoke to her. I do not know how long they spoke, but when they came back down, he prayed for everybody, smiled, and went about his day. Mama was by his side.

The house continued to entertain, or more so, swallow people with a cloud of death that hung above it. I felt like that day, death had its wings spread high and wide, and it was enjoying every minute of it. Where was God through all of this? I called my aunt's phone several more times, but still no answer.

"Sugar, please go and eat," my mother said. I just stared at her straight-faced by the sink. Seconds went by, and then it happened, fresh new tears tasting as salty as the ocean began to fall down my face again. How could she leave like this? She really could not be gone. What about everyone here?

I told her to call her, but she didn't call her. She did not call her because she was confirming her death. This was just one thing I wanted her to do: call her and speak to her because she just could not be dead; at about 6 pm, I was still in strong denial that there was no way that my aunt could be dead. This is nearly 24 hours, but it doesn't make a difference to me. Miracles happen in the Bible all the time, so there is no reason why a miracle couldn't happen in this case. I was in the mindset that if He did it before, He could do it again. Did Jesus not raise Lazarus from the grave? What about the sick who became well? There were people in the Bible who had leprosy that were banned from the city and had to create a sort of leprosy camp, and even they were delivered and allowed to return to their loved ones. You can only imagine how I questioned what was happening at the moment, and it was only day one.

It was only day one, and I was already completely mentally out of it. This had never happened before and would now be the catalyst for the next decade. Why not something else Lord? I wanted nothing to do with anybody or any faith if it was not going to bring my aunt back. I even gave it three days because I mean, Jesus brought the dead back to life days later, right after the body was rotting. He breathed life right back into it. Death had me spiraling. My irrational thoughts had irrational thoughts, and yet, Friday passed, Saturday passed, and Sunday passed, and still nothing happened. I had to be strong. I had to keep it together. Internally, I was just not understanding. I did not understand this whole faith that everybody was talking about. I did not understand the better place she was in. With all the private school education and church background, it didn't click. Did she say she wanted to go there? I never received a message. She could have told us or maybe prepared us. Nope, she just decided to leave on her own.

I wasn't aware at the moment, but I was operating through the five stages of grief. Within the weeks to come, my mood suddenly went from grief and sadness to total bitterness and anger. I was angry with a dead person. I threw away all knowledge of faith because, for all I know, I could not see the beauty of God in this situation. I was still going to church, I was still an usher, but I was not present. I was not receiving from God or anybody what was meant to be for me at this point in life. It would take months before I began to understand and do a 180 on the faithfulness of God. It would be months before I would smile again. The mask was painted on perfectly, and as long as people thought I was fine, I would not be questioned. Allow the role, and that is for me to be the strong, perfect child that everybody thought I was and I would perform. I would receive an Oscar. I would be allowed to entertain my thoughts and questions, occasionally seeking God, but when He did not answer, I would go silent again. I would turn to the world because the world I could see, the world I could get answers quickly. Sometimes, I gave Him the benefit of the doubt, trying to find the right verse to find peace, but nothing. I never received the explanation that day as to why all this was happening, not knowing it was only the beginning of a long journey that would shape out to be my faith.

The month of September finally ended. It was a month full of tears, questions, anger, hatred, and more. I returned to school a week after her death and tried to make up all the work I missed, but nothing was registering. As my family slowly slipped away, my grades began to slip too. However, I couldn't let that be known. I had a role to uphold. I had to remain perfect and level in all aspects. This wasn't a role assigned to me, but one that I put on myself, maybe because I was the oldest, perhaps I cared about my image, maybe it was pride, maybe I was scared. But I couldn't let anyone worry about me or ask questions. I had to be strong. It was not at all easy, but I kept pushing. I pushed through without direction, not knowing what to do with my life. Twelve months ago, I started a new journey excited, eager, and ready. Now, I never hated the way I did the next couple of months.

Everything and everybody that crossed my path did not sit well with me. They weren't her, so what was the point? I just went numb, doing things because I had to, not because I wanted to. There wasn't anything that I wanted to do except be angry. I wanted answers, and I wanted them now. I needed her back to me, and every day, I would wait for the stupid joke to be over, but it wasn't. So, every day, I became angrier, immune to the mundane ways of the world because they had no effect on me any longer. In my mourning, I officially withdrew from Howard University.

Chapter Three

A few weeks after my aunt's death, I walked into the School of Business and the Office of the Registrar and went through the short but formal process to no longer be a student at the university. My mom had no clue I would do such; even that morning, I didn't think I would go through with it. However, when I boarded that train and transferred stops, I knew I could not sustain this emotionally, and my parents could not sustain it financially. It was not supposed to be this hard. I finished the rest of the semester once again close to academic probation, this time failing two classes, yet I could've cared less. I was alone. I was tired. I was finished. My journey to being like Joan Clayton had come to a halt, and I had no plan B in sight.

I was unaware of my purpose and did not know which direction I was headed. I didn't care which direction I was headed. People handle death in different ways at different moments. In the current season that I was in, my aunt's death was taking me on a downward spiral of what I felt would be my own. My aunt's death wasn't the only death I experienced that year. The irony of life is that the aunt, who was the first person at our door as soon as the news of death broke in my house, would lose her husband two months later. A man who was sitting in our kitchen at the dining table, providing comfort to our family, was now gone. He was a man I grew to respect in how he led his family and the church and held respect for the youth. Someone who was always around was now gone just like that. That is another death that plays in my head on occasion like it had just happened. Death would appear again on a bright day in the holiday season; instead of darkness coming over, the sun shined extremely bright as if to mock us all.

When one gains a little sliver of normalcy and peace, it is interesting how the devil quickly consumes it once again. Or was it God adding more problems to a test that I obviously could not complete? I did not understand the next series of events; all I knew was that I now began to question things even more. I had lost an aunt, and now, the day after Thanksgiving, a day to be thankful and all, I got the news that I had lost a dear family friend. Like I said, whether you prepared or not, this was the shock of the year for me, a fresh crack in me that would soon break. He was not sick, and there was no accident. He just passed away from "natural causes." A death I prepared for hurt terribly, and now one I didn't expect; how was I to feel? I had, in a way, prepared for Auntie. I watched her die, still holding on to a little piece of faith that I felt was there. This death, this was just not correct, unnatural, just plain mean. I was beyond myself to understand what had just happened.

For a while, I would question the brightest of days because two times now, they had signified death, and I couldn't take it anymore—

bright days filled with tears and condolences. People who came and consoled me, I, in turn, now had to console them. You know they say death comes in threes. A few weeks, perhaps months, would go by, and I would hear of another death, this one not close to me, but for this little boy, I prayed. I remember praying in the basement when no one could hear me but God. I begged for God to heal him. I prayed for him to get off life support. I did not know him, but I knew I didn't want him to die. I didn't want another family mourning, but unfortunately, He also died. My prayers weren't working, so I quit praying.

That week and the ones to come quickly became a repeat of the tears unsuppressed. Tears that nobody ever saw, tears that nobody ever knew. I didn't feel like it was safe to show emotion. I had to be strong. I was alone in my strength. I couldn't afford to wear my emotions on my sleeves or properly express how I felt, so I began to submerse myself. The seeds planted were being fertilized with grief, leaving no room for growth or healing, buried in sorrow. With the last few weeks of the semester closing in on me, I kept to myself and did what I could to get myself back on track. I now know that in those moments when I ran to try and catch my train or felt a heavy heart, God must've been holding on to me harder than I imagined. I couldn't have made it through without His grip on me. As much as I pulled away on the inside, He had me covered. I felt completely alone, surrounded but ultimately alone.

I grew into this monotonous lifestyle of school and trains and tears. I had plans to attend university, finish in four years, get a good job in a big city, and live life well. Yet, here I was, and I couldn't even get through the first half of it. I had no more to give, no will, no emotion, no aunt, no uncle, no degree pending. Honestly, there was no fighting I could do. It was time for me to go, not go and die, just go. I was untethered to life, operating with no plan.

I love how God shows up with His Word right on time. There was so much happening in the weeks to come and the months to follow after my aunt. I wasn't looking to remember God, but He saw fit to remember me, and in that, I would have the verse that would anchor me for the next ten years. Jer 29:11 "For I know the thoughts that I think toward you," says Yahweh, "thoughts of peace, and not of evil, to give you hope and a future."

With the will I had left, this verse anchored me. I understand when some churches say they have an anchor scripture for the year, month, or season. In this life, what are you anchored to? I wasn't even 20 yet, but I knew this verse would carry me through the next decade. I found myself coming back to this verse multiple times. Before it became the verse on every IG profile, I had it in my heart. Before I switched churches and saw it was the anchor scripture for that church, I had it in my heart. I mean, it was on my wall. I had mugs, frames, everything. I needed to believe that God would not leave me in grief and on a desolate land. I had to prosper. I had to have hope and a future. I had to believe He would be faithful despite what everything was looking like.

…….

A Garden in Bloom

A part of the future that I had imagined for myself was thinking that I would find my college sweetheart and fall in love. I dreamed of meeting him on The Yard, a Love and Basketball, Dwayne and Whitley-type scenario. I have always been a lover girl at heart. I believed in Disney love, the Prince Charming love, and the happily ever after. I have probably seen or heard 80% of the RomComs made, and I go head over heels each time, tears forming. I didn't go the high school sweetheart route because I wasn't even allowed to date in high school, even though I did once. I figured college would be the time to shine. I wanted it to be part of my college story, imagining myself as a lawyer in a big city with my career-driven black man. I imagined "couple goals" before there were even "couple goals" to use as a hashtag. That is a storyline I would go for. I believed in something I didn't grow up with because I trusted it to be possible, even if it was tainted and idealistic. I believed in marriage and love. Time, wisdom, and understanding would help me later discern what love was and what it was to love like Christ. I can say now that for a while and for the months to come, I was operating with other emotions and not a very clear head. Folks will say lust; folks will say like. I will say that grief and immaturity will have you do wild things.

It did not start that way. A month after my aunt's diagnosis, May, we were all still full of hope, so life continued semi-normal. In preparation for a church celebration, I found myself on a one-hour road trip to pick up meat pies and puff puffs at my place. He was the only one who could drive, and my house held the snacks. I remember my friend asking to come along, but an auntie said no, that we two would go and come back. She should have had her come along. However, from that drive and the weeks to come, it was a good time. Conversations were light, and summer was full of group moments when possible. But life takes a turn when you least expect it, and now your heart is involved, so it hurts even more. Everyone has their vice. I didn't do drugs or alcohol, and I wasn't having sex, but I needed his attention. He was the last guy my aunt ever knew of. How amazing would it have been to know that she died but still knew who I would marry? How much delusion did I have in my tea that month?

In the midst of all that was happening, I found myself wrapped up in a "will they, won't they" trope of a situation for three years. Summer was over, and the realities of death and poor communication created murky waters for a possible relationship to swim in. That was not a storyline I enjoyed for myself. I needed something, someone to hold on to, that made sense and offered an escape. He was my escape without being asked. I had no business with him. I had no reason to chase potential, no reason to chase physical desires, no reason to compromise my being, and no reason to lose myself when I had already lost so much. However, he was also a friend. Before the will they won't they, he was a friend I had known for a very long time, and our friendship was also taking a hit. I get why they say you can never go back once you cross a line with a friend. Life was dealing with us both in different ways and clinging to each other was not helping, especially if I was doing the clinging. I was clinging to a sinking ship. I often wonder, if death didn't happen right when things were starting to form, would it have worked out? The makings of such a storyline were right there. He was the end of my teenage years and the beginning of my twenties, so I kept holding on. He was also my friend first. Yet, sometimes, we hold ourselves in a position where we miss out on true healthy relationships. I will say it for the person wondering right now: let it go, go, and grow. Go and heal.

....

I had to have hope that I would still have a degree in my hands in 4 years. My plan wasn't to be a dropout. I had no skill or trade to fall back on, so I needed the degree. I still owed the illustrious Howard University $6,000, and with no payment in sight, there was also no transcript, meaning there was no university near or far I could enroll in. I should have thought my withdrawal through because I thought I could go ahead and jump on another campus, but it wasn't that simple. Time was running out, and this was all new to me and everyone around me. I had enrolled in Community College during the winter break to knock out a fitness elective, and with further questions, I learned I could get credits there until I figured out how to transfer elsewhere. So, my next journey began.

Being in community college would be the reset that I needed. What I appreciated most during my time there was the opportunity for success for all levels. You see, at most four years, everyone is the same age and has a similar mindset and goals, which is not good or bad. Yet, there was an ease of knowing that whether my classmate was 18 or 41, we all just wanted to do better. We wanted to be better. I needed this place to regain myself and strategize without an obscene amount of tuition or a cross-state road trip in my way. I've often realized that some problems are not problems when you take out factors within your control and zero in. So my mom and I made a plan that I would get all the credits I could while I could, we would get the $6,000, and I would be out in 4 years. This wasn't going to be too bad, and now I finally got my license; technically, I was forced to get my license because I was getting too comfortable with public transit, but things were taking an upswing.

The last nine months had me on a ride, and I was happy to report I was still buckled in. In a matter of months, I had been shown a new understanding of resilience. Don't let them see you sweat. Always keep pushing. Keep focused. Remember Jeremiah 29:11 and the plans of the Lord. When it was all said and done, I left the age of 19 feeling beaten but not broken. To list all that I lost at that age would be redundant. Understanding of what was gained was still to be searched for. Now, it was time for a new decade, and there is so much to be said about your twenties. The end of 19 planted me right where I had no desire to be, but where faith would have no choice but to take root and show me the beauty of what would be the next ten years when looked at through God's eyes.

I want to say that I came into my twenties with high hopes, but don't we all? The twenties are the years when you get the degree, the job, the business, the husband, the house, and the 2.5 kids; at least, that's what I thought anyway. That's what I imagined in my head, but where was any of it? To quote Elle Varner, "Now in my twenties, all that matters is sex, cars, and money; I ain't got none of the three."

Chapter Four

I was entering my twenties with still no plan in sight. The planner in me had no plan. The spring I turned 20, I finished one semester in community college and was re-enrolling for another because I still could not get my transcript released from Howard. I was running out of classes though. I was also running out of patience, getting the run around from the same guy because I was still chasing the potential of a 90's love story. I had been free from the numbness of grief from the winter season and was beginning to live again and was serving in my church, still holding on to what I thought was faith but, in truth, was responsibility. I have heard it said that your twenties could be your "live, laugh, and love years," but I believe that is only if you make an effort to create it. I had to find ways to live, laugh, and love in the uncertainty, and I dare say I was pushing along.

I was now in my twenties with no clarity in sight, but I knew these were the years to get things done. These were the years when we were finally free to do whatever we wanted and be whoever we wanted. In just a few years, I could have the house, the car, the 2.5 kids, and the man of my dreams, which would be a piece of the dream if I stayed the course. It would all make sense, working in my corporate career, an office on the horizon, and making everyone proud, just as I had done many times before. My imagination and thoughts had truly gotten the best of me, but by now, understand that I've always seen life with a picturesque view. I just had to get over the current hump, and everything would happen. At the same time, as I was creating plans for what I thought I needed and what the world taught me I wanted, God had plans of His own, as we remember Jeremiah 29:11 and Proverbs 16:9, which says, "A man's heart plans his course, but Yahweh directs his steps."

I didn't just hear about God for the first time when I turned 20, I grew up in the church, multiple churches. I went to Private Christian schools for most of my early academic years. I knew the songs, the verses, and the culture of the church, and because I followed the rules, my life, for the most part growing up, represented someone that I suppose from the outside looking in went to church and was a Christian. Even when I did things I knew were wrong, I still heard a small voice. I may not have listened, but I heard it. It wasn't a moral compass because, many times, a moral compass will cover a grey area, a safe zone. This was a black and white clear voice. When I turned 20, that voice seemed to get louder. I began to get restless and uncomfortable with how I lived, and it started in my environment. This is when I began to realize how important that company kept matters. This is why it is important to take a moment to honor the friends who helped you grow, even if they think they didn't.

I had a friend staying with me at the time, also going through her things, and during it all, I watched her draw near to Christ. Still swimming in waves of anger with the cards being dealt in my life and its frustrations, I watched her change. She would wake up early and read the Bible, set time aside, and be in the Word or have prayer. What was this constant quiet time? What was this new relationship? Why was it happening constantly in my space?

I looked at her like she was crazy. I didn't feel it had to be that deep. I drove her out of the room because of my words and anger, like she was doing too much. I didn't understand that she was just starting to scratch the surface. What we both didn't know back then was that she was watering the seeds that had been planted in my life. Well, I thank God for her obedience. I understand that there must be people positioned for you to move. I can't say I would have felt the desire if it wasn't always around.

Was I impressionable? Or was God using her to press on my heart? We were both ushers in the church, but there was a zeal to her praise and her worship, and I wanted it. Watching someone go through life and still hold faith was awe-inspiring. I wanted to know that even through the shaking, the anchor of the Lord would hold me steady like it looked to be keeping her. However, I felt I wouldn't get it where I was currently worshiping. There was too much history, distraction, temptation. I needed to remove myself and make room for only God. I needed to cut ties.

I needed a fresh word, a new word, a now word. So, I began at a new church, and it was different. In all my years, I had never seen so many young people wanting to be active in faith. It was weird, but for me, it was necessary. Nothing else was working at the time, so it was time to make some positive changes. I needed my life to move in a direction that made sense. Dare I say that life began to take an upswing from this point.

That summer, I felt as if I had met God for the first time. I wish I could bottle that feeling up; it was euphoric. There is something electric and full about taking every care, worry, concern, good and bad, and just giving it to God. That summer, I trusted God and had complete faith that everything would be ok. I understood the zeal that my friend had. I remember my first Bible plan on August 7th, 2014, called "Working Through Anger." I said if I'm going to do this right, I can't be angry anymore, not with death, not about college, and definitely not about no man. I felt free. I held on to that freedom. I took that freedom and began to make YouTube videos. I wanted everyone to experience what I was feeling because of God. I was on a spiritual high. The Gaithers wrote a popular song: "Because He Lives, I can face tomorrow." I was facing each day head first.

My YouTube era was short-lived. YouTube takes a strong level of commitment. However, I was learning my voice and allowing myself to be seen and heard. I gave myself discomfort so others could get comfortable with faith. I wanted to be all in. The beauty of faith is when you first come into it, you are all in and eager, like the children spoken of in Matthew 18:2. That is the time when you don't care what anyone says or how things look as long as people see God.

That is where I was. After months of pain and frustration, I needed everyone to know the joy and understand how I got it.

The thing you find out for yourself is the amount of surrender and vulnerability that comes with talking about faith, especially on video. I wasn't ready. I wasn't secure in my boldness. I kept my faith in a bottle that if you wanted some, I would pour it out, but I wasn't just going to leave it open and let it get stale. I was operating on my strength. I was still monitoring the parts of me to expose and keep hidden. I did not think I could be camera-facing. I did not think anybody wanted to see me or hear me. Mind torment is a detriment by itself, but we'll get to that, and at the end of the day, YouTube wasn't the route to take.

What I put out on video or kept did not serve as a measure of how much of a believer I was. I knew that in my heart, but my actions were not aligned, even though I had faith. I found my footing and began serving at my new church shortly after. I started working at the mall, not the road to corporate America, but there was income coming in. There was truly good news and miracles all around because not only was I enrolled once more in community college, but it would be my last semester. It is a miracle that cannot be unpacked to this day, but let's just say I got my transcript, and not a dime was paid by me. I printed out several copies because I didn't want any issues in case the system closed again, but I got my transcript, applied, and was accepted into a 4-year university. God was moving and with speed on my behalf. I was full of joy. I was seeing the evidence of who God was, and yet I became more aware of who I still was in the midst of it all. Fully imperfect.

I was still watching Bad Girls Club and still found myself with desires and thoughts that were not of God. I still found myself seeking validation from all the wrong people. I didn't find God and become perfect because that's never usually how it goes. There were things I did not yet have convictions about and situations and habits that would prove to still have more pull in my actions than the faith that was still growing. I was operating on rocky soil, and situations had a way of tipping you over.

When I got to Towson University, I thought, "3 more semesters, and I'm out of here." I thought, " Yes, God had answered a prayer," and He did, but a different path was being taken that would ultimately require different prayers from the first. After having my credits transferred and being in a position to begin working towards graduation, I sat down with my counselor. We reviewed all the information she had on me, and she told me I would not be graduating in the spring of 2016. I felt my whole world shift, which now may not be a big deal big picture, but in that moment, I felt like a failure. She told me that I did not have the prerequisites to enter the major and would have to graduate a year later. That was not possible, and there was no way I could do that. She told me the closest I could get would be the fall of 2016 if I took classes year-round, and so I did. I didn't have a winter or summer break and barely a spring break. I took any class they allowed and I needed. This time around, there was no exploring, no parties, and no extracurriculars. I just wanted to graduate and not look back. You get a prayer, and there's still somewhat of a fine print attached, but the fine print is also for something better, even if we don't see it yet. Her telling me I had an extra semester was a slow-moving tipping point.

. . . .

I turned 21 the year I transferred. I don't remember much about my 21st birthday. I didn't throw a party or go out and get drunk. I had a final exam that day at 8 am. That year I also got a dog, the best present to date. I remember that summer. I remember failing my accounting class and thinking, "Why was this even my major?" I remember questioning everything but not doing anything about it because I was already two years into it. I also remember returning to the half-relationship that I thought I had gotten out of. I told you it was three years of confusion. I remember almost losing my purity, something that I now hold so dear. I remember the late-night conversations and sweet nothings that were fed in my most vulnerable state of emotions and uncertainty. I thought surely this time he was serious, but it takes two.

Everyone saw us, some were rooting for us, and we were older, so the decisions made sense. However, our bodies still spoke louder than our words. But not a day goes by where I am not grateful for what God ripped me out of. The lust, the temptation, the shame, and the confusion would go on to follow me for several years before I felt free. But I still had my purity, and for that, I slept easy. The summer I turned 21, I felt like I kept falling into one black hole, and then God would pull me out, and I would fall again, knowingly, and God would pull me out, always by my side in my mess, still shining on me. It would be many years before I let another man get to know me again, pursue me again, and for me to understand my worth again. This guy wasn't a bad guy and didn't do any damage, but what I learned that summer let me know that God was for me and always by me, with the best of the best in mind.

.....

That fall, I took all the mess, emotions, and confusion and allowed God to use me through words this time. Believe it or not, this book would not be my first rodeo. The love of reading, writing, and literature has been in my blood from birth, but when it's not what others agree on, you tend to shy away from participating; at least, that's what I did. I created a blog, but nobody really knew about it for a while. I treated it like a mystery writer situation. I would write and sometimes share through social media, but other times, not at all, and I figured whoever needed to see it would see. Gifts I was scared to embrace, light that I was trying to hide.

My friends who knew encouraged me to continue writing and sharing my work, always the supportive ones they were, but even still, I was in my head. For some time, I was consistent, but fear, my image; I couldn't possibly let people know my thoughts. The posts became inconsistent, and college was getting the better of me. Eventually, that would fall by the wayside, just like YouTube. Was it possible to share God without sharing a bit of yourself? I was trying to do that, and it wasn't working, so I went with share nothing; that was my default. I did it well, and if you didn't know me, you really didn't know I was doing it. How do you say...Mysterious? Or maybe selfish, depending on who you asked and how many souls we should be saving.

Although I don't remember my 21st birthday or, honestly, many things from that "monumental" age of adulthood, I remember going back to Texas for the first time since the funeral that winter. This would be my first time there by myself without my aunt there. I remember when she had passed, telling myself I would never go back there again; now and then, I catch myself still saying I won't go back, but those were just emotions and inconsideration talking. I had family there, after all. So I entered the new year with my family in Dallas, yet without one crucial member, it was trippy. I felt like I was back in time. Everything was exactly as it was before she passed; it felt like she had just stepped out to get groceries or something. I would come to learn that everyone has their way of dealing with grief, and I suppose for my cousins, this was their way. The visit didn't heal me in any way, but it was necessary, and sometimes in life, you have to do things that are necessary at the moment and get clarity in the future, or not at all. That's how things are at times. Into a new year I came, roots forming, soil leveled.

Chapter Five

The beginning of the year would prove to truly be a time of moments when I was at peace. I was, for once, just simply happy with where life was going. I was boldly strolling into the new year with a taste of rest. I knew I was almost done with school and was ready to enjoy all that life had to offer, putting the college years behind me. I was going to make 2016 my year, no matter what. I would enjoy and hold on to this God-given peace for however long I could. My mind was at ease. My thoughts were clear. Philippians 4:8 says, "Finally, brothers, whatever things are true, whatever things are honorable, whatever things are just, whatever things are pure, whatever things are lovely, whatever things are of good report: if there is any virtue and if there is any praise, think about these things." That verse, along with Jeremiah 29:11, became the catalyst to what would become the best year of my college career, not simply because of graduation to come. I intended to celebrate from beginning to end.

A lot of life up to this point had been a rollercoaster of faith, relationships, and goals with no seatbelt. Finally, I was enjoying the lazy river of life for a bit. I began to see the world, and I felt like expectations were being dropped. I could begin to live freely as created. This is the year I found myself soaking in the sweet sun from Old San Juan and enjoying the sand in Montego Bay. This is the year that ol' boy said, "Have a nice life," and in every way, I did. My hair was growing out naturally as I finally caved and gave it to a little snip. I was full of joy, and my mouth was full of laughter. I was starting to give *Stella Got Her Groove Back*, minus the younger man, well, minus any man, to be honest. This is the year I was fully submitted in faith and with all my mess, even though I didn't feel ready. I got baptized, publicly saying I belonged to the Lord. Even in that public moment, I remember not feeling ready, but then a friend reminded me that I would never be ready, and it wasn't about me. I took that step. I was allowing myself to be full of joy, experience peace, and let God in again. I was allowing myself to take root.

But all of that would not come without its moments of heaviness. I was finally almost done with the degree and would rid myself of academia. The irony of life is that as a young child, I absolutely loved learning and reading and thoroughly enjoyed school. My college journey turned me off so badly that it would be years before that same love returned to me again. So, I was almost done with my degree, and while that would be a joy for many, for me, it brought bouts of sadness. The first bout appeared in the spring. The reminder that I was supposed to be in the spring graduating class rang out loud as I watched all my friends and colleagues cross the stage ahead of me. It hurt even more watching my class from HU because I would never see my name under an HU degree, and I would NEVER have

Obama speak at my commencement ceremony. I wanted to run into a wall. What a full circle moment it would have been to be a part of such a historic graduation when, freshman year, I helped to vote him into his second term, marching in the freeze of the morning to hear his inauguration speech with my floormates. This may seem small, but for me, those full-circle moments were a big deal, left empty because I had to leave. The whole month of May, while I celebrated and rejoiced with others, I beat myself up because, in a way, I failed. Nobody would ever tell me that I failed, but I know this is not what my parents had in mind for me. However, living for my parents is not what God had for me, and at 22, I was still yet to learn how to separate the two.

Bout number two would come the following semester. When it was my turn to be celebrated, it felt like everything was against me down to the last final exam. In my final semester, I had no choice but to hold on to Jer 29:11. As I applied for job after job and received rejection after rejection, I felt myself withering away. Exams were not getting easier. I had quit working at the mall to focus, and now I was out of money, and I was losing myself to imposter syndrome and comparison. Life was swallowing me bit by bit. I couldn't handle the pressure, and my skin couldn't handle it, but thank God for shea butter.

I was not alone and yet felt I had nowhere to release the emotions and stress. I was losing weight, and I was scared. I could not afford to fail anything anymore. I didn't know what was next. I didn't have a game plan in sight. I was applying for jobs anywhere and everywhere. I considered the Peace Corps, but I didn't want to leave my dog for two years (literally, she was the only reason I stayed).

I felt like I was moving like a ship without a sail. I held on to The Word, yet I felt life spinning me in circles. It's easy to say now that senior year and everything that makes up the college experience were not a big deal. Those are just small moments in your life, especially if you only do undergrad; so much more happens in your twenties. But for anyone at that age, in that moment, their emotions are not to be diminished. It is all they know; for me, it was all I knew. If I didn't have a plan or job in the next few weeks, I was hopeless. Yes, I am that dramatic. I was still considering law school and preparing for the LSAT, so there was that pressure. Should I get a master's degree instead? What life was I making for myself? I honestly did not know.

But I was still getting to know God. And when it was all said and done, when I crossed that stage with no job in sight, I knew He had big plans for me. I knew that wherever He was taking me had to be bigger than me because I had nothing left to plan. So I graduated in December, and one month later, after our annual 21-day fast, He reminded me of His word, and I began my first role in corporate America.

The faithfulness of God never left me. The past four years were full of planted seeds that were starting to manifest and would continue, as the years went on, to reveal the nature of God and His love. But you see, just as I believe the Lord planted seeds, there would be some seeds also planted by the enemy that I would have to uproot. If you've ever planted anything, you would know that a seed needs to be fully covered in soil to be in an environment of growth. I thought I was leaving college fully covered, but my roots were still exposed and would produce some weak leaves unable to weather what lay ahead until I replanted on good soil.

Part Two: The Seedling

"A friend loves at all time; and a brother is born for adversity."

- Proverbs 17:17

Chapter Six

The college years are cute, they are fun, they are challenging in their own right, and despite all the doom and gloom that came through during those years for me, I made it out. I made it out with a degree and a job not long after, so I can say I wasn't doing terribly for myself. I wasn't strolling through NYC with a briefcase in hand and had no plans to return for another degree, but I wasn't lacking either. However, the years that follow college are honestly not what is to be expected. Who is actually to say what's next? And therein lies the beginning of a different view of life as we know it. The ball is in your court, and what we choose to do from here on out is on us. There is no road map. The milestones are grey, and yet, we begin to slowly hold ourselves up to these standards that come from the abyss. We start to let different goals, things, and circumstances weigh on us, and not once do we remember to ask God, "What do we do now?"At least let me speak for myself.

I say this often, but preparing for adulthood with any set schedule is null and void. Not all of us, but many of us live this life where, for 18 years, we know when to wake up and eat lunch, we see the same community of people whether it be in class, neighborhood, church, babysitters, or the local mailman. We all, for the most part, graduate at the same pace. Even if some folks switch schools, you still have the same life structure. The milestones make sense, our routines are set, and there is very little grey. May I be so bold to say that these are the years we can foolishly boast about ourselves because God has given us an order of things? And then we go into college thinking, "Oh boy, freedom! I can set my schedule. I'm 18, and I can play the lottery. I'm over 21, and I can drink. I'm an adult." And yet, we are still in a way in a bubble of similar points in life. One foot in the certainty of college, a trade, or an inherited business, the other foot waiting to make a name on your own, tethered no more to anything or anyone. It is just a matter of when. Then we graduate, we reach the next milestone, and suddenly, a celebratory time filled with more unknowns than we have ever had. The safety net of friendships, meal plans, Johnny down the street, that trusted restaurant with your go-to order all changes.

Friends move, folks get married, folks get new jobs, and some get "left behind" in school and life. None of it can you truly prepare for; it just happens. The invitations arrive, the homes are built, and the goodbye parties are had. Life begins to move at a pace, and you have to wonder if you are moving with it or if it is all just moving around you. What are you doing? This isn't to say that all of these changes do not happen in our formative years, but instead, there is something less grounding and uncertain post-college that leaves one untethered to life. And then it is at that moment we choose to remember God.

Not all days, 24/7, as He says we should, but when we don't know what to do next.

Life post-grad was full of layers. Who was I outside of school? What kind of adult did I want to be? I had no real concrete idea. Everything I thought I knew and planned the last four years had hit the fan, so to plan the rest would be bold. One thing I did know was that I was a good friend, but remaining that same person on new terrain would prove difficult. I found myself, very early on, tackling the layer of adult friendships. Much like the routines that we all grew up to have, many of our friends came the same way, and now, with no more milestones to tackle at the same time, we all begin different journeys. Where do our friends fall in that?

In the beginning, you don't notice it; the calls, brunches, events, and schedules are still available, and everyone is still trying to show up. Over time, interests and commonalities change, time apart increases, and the level of intentionality decreases. Intentionality is the word everyone throws around, yet no one catches it. That was me in early post-grad. As I watched things change, I tried hard to remain intentional with the relationships I had formed in college, even as a freshman, but the truth is that it wasn't being caught. Often, a lack of intentionality in a relationship is not one person's fault or another. It's just time for a change. I heard it once said by a pastor, " You have friends for a season, a reason, and a lifetime." Embrace the friendships for what they are during that time, and if they must leave, it's also ok.

A Garden in Bloom

I had to learn not to pour out of an empty cup all in the name of friendship; otherwise, I would come up empty. I had to learn to make room for those willing to catch and return the friendship I had to bring. We meet so many people in our twenties, and we are even reintroduced to some, which can be exciting. With that, we introduce different versions of ourselves, and only some get the privilege of knowing the full us.

Chapter Seven

O f all the ships that set sail, avoid the situationship, prepare in due time for the relationship if one so desires, but get on the friendship so you remain out of the sea. I quickly learned how much more of a necessity friendships were in adulthood and how they should be of quality and not necessarily quantity. I used to think the more friends you had, the more you had people for everything. They showed up, and popularity was key, but that isn't the case. You can't social climb your way through life, and around me, it felt like many were worried about their social currency rather than any other. Ironically, it has frequently been reported on different news outlets in recent years that there is a loneliness epidemic, especially among young adults. I would think not because there aren't enough people, but rather the quality of people who are showing up for one another. Clearly, with all the people in the world, many of us are operating with an emotional deficit.

A common thing the body of Christ or places with them have said is, "Don't do life alone." Yet, everyone is one foot in and one foot out of relationships, not rooted, and in a cycle, feeling lonely or uneasy about relationships. The Word of God says in Genesis 2:18, "

It is not good for the man to be alone." Right from the beginning, God knows that we should not be alone. I think He not only meant that in a romantic way, but wholistically. I did not want that to be me, coming in and out of friendships with no depth. I needed people that I would carry and would carry me along in these years because it works both ways. Finding friends isn't always hard; it's the vulnerability, accountability, and actions that many struggle with. Coming out of a space where many friends were served on a platter for us (school), the accountability and actions would change a bit for some of us. As I was coming into my own, I wondered if who I was becoming would still work for the friendships that I had.

2017 was, without a doubt, in my mind, the Best Summer Ever. Culture often looks back at 2016 because of the music and what have you, but 2017, for me, solidified the beauty of what adult friendships could be and have been, and also the importance of fellowship with like-minded people. At 23 years of age, I was shown the beauty of sisterhood with like-minded people, and a time was had. This notion of women who are Believers being boring, stuffy, or rigid is a lie from the pit of hell. I will remember the summer of 2017 as the best summer of all my twenties. Nothing remarkable was done, but laughter and joy covered our mouths daily. We sought out and found the Lord in new territory. We climbed literal mountains and got lost for 7 miles. We escaped to pretty waterfalls. We ended up in a music video. We went on road trips to new cities, looked cute, fellowshipped, and ate to our heart's content—all of this we did together. Living life fully and out loud with a sound community is beautiful. Most of these women would continue to be with me throughout my life, and some wouldn't. But again, it's ok because the depth of that friendship season still watered my roots for today. It is important where you are rooted. Roots provide an anchor. They help with growth, and only in the proper environment can roots allow a plant to grow tall; because of these women, I was starting to grow.

It is true that you find your lifelong friends in college, uniquely shared experiences bringing you together. However, you never stop meeting people, and the right people, whenever you both meet, never leave from that point on. In the early stages of my twenties, even with the beautiful friendships that I was being blessed with, I found myself jumping from one friendship to the next, trying to figure out where we were headed and if we had to all be going in the same direction. I knew I wasn't a social climber and couldn't keep all the friendships the same, but I was confused. Was there a right way?

I was having trouble letting some people go because as much as I understood its importance, I'm of the "we grew up together" mentality, which can be to our detriment at times. It's hard watching everyone grow into themselves and not knowing what's next for you. It's also harder to watch yourself change and realize you can't carry others along with you. The access stops here. People change, and we are all supposed to, at some point, be held accountable for how we change. Proverbs 18:24 says, " A man of many companions may be ruined, but there is a friend who sticks closer than a brother." Still figuring things out and still unsure about a lot, one thing for certain was I knew I would not come to ruin for anybody. Woman of faith or not, that's a proverb of common sense, which is not common for many. Make it common for you. We choose our friends, even more so as adults. It's important who we carry along with us.

I tried to carry everyone with me; remember, I said I struggle with letting go. I remember always being the friend that would show up and check in, "just thinking of you," and I still am with wisdom. The friend that would drive hours and be on time. I had a friend once use the term "designer friend" on herself. I said, wow, I am genuinely a top-notch designer and an elite, one-of-a-kind friend, and yet I was pouring out of an empty cup.

I remember asking God if there was something wrong with me that people don't think of me as much as I think of them. Call it a gift, but who said I wanted this? It is difficult seeing people without being seen, and for a long time, that's how I felt. Even with quality around me, a voice would still say it was not enough, making me feel empty and making me feel like in a growing world of branding and influencing, I needed to have something for people to check in on rather than just my being. I had to be doing. But I had nothing I wanted to do than just be.

I understand that comparison is the thief of joy, but there are times when you cannot help yourself, and it lingers. Post-undergrad life presents itself as one of those opportune times, depending on where you are and who you are. Call me immature, but hey, science says the brain doesn't fully develop until our mid-twenties, and at 23 years old, I wanted my friendships to look like an episode of

Girlfriends before it all went south with Joan and Toni. Yet, everything you try and think you know about friendship and sisterhood doesn't show up the way movies and shows paint the picture of togetherness. That's just not the case.

I knew this wasn't high school or college anymore, but because some of the maturity levels of folks were still there I thought surely the friendships may not change. People change. I changed. Big life moments happen that make or break friendships. I witnessed many moments of " it didn't have to end like that." After a few of those moments, I learned the quickest prayer that God would answer for me would be to remove people from my life, especially if they drew me away from Him, and especially to avoid the heartbreak of friendship. I couldn't handle drama and shouldn't have to when my Father could make it go away. When He first answers the prayer, you are like wait a second, bring them back, but then your vision changes, and then you are like, I get it now, and it's ok.

I began to cover my friendships in prayer, the same way I prayed for my spouse. I prayed for my friends even more. The environment had to be good for each of us to grow, and if there was a weed, it had to be pulled out with love. God wants us to be in deep, fruitful friendships. Ecclesiastes 4:12 says, " If a man prevails against one who is alone...and a threefold cord is not quickly broken." This verse is often used for marriages but was actually written in the context of friendship! We are meant to build each other up, cover, defend, and love each other.

A Garden in Bloom

There may not be too many friendships examined in the Bible like that of David and Jonathan, but a unique one I think of from time to time is that of Mary and Elizabeth. Although the Bible says they were cousins, they were also friends. Mary, being much younger than Elizabeth, related once more as they both found themselves in similar situations. Both women were chosen by God to carry children that would change the world. So, with the special task at hand, they walked with each other. They both understood what the other needed in that season of waiting, rejoicing, fear, and maybe even grief. We don't know the depths of their friendship, but we can read in Luke 1 verses 38-56 that Elizabeth was happy for Mary. She called her blessed and rejoiced with her. She never left her side, even when others didn't understand or believe. Together, they held on to the words God gave them individually and watched them come to pass. I believe that even in the small section of that chapter God showcases the importance of showing up and being there for one another. Going back to Ecclesiastes 4:9-12 "Two are better than one because they have a good reward on their labor." To be literal, Elizabeth and Mary had the best return on labor in the history of all labor and delivery, as far as I'm concerned. The verse continues, "… but woe to him who is alone when he falls, and doesn't have another to lift him up."

There is nothing too big or too small that I have not been able to share with those closest to me. There is also nothing too big or small that they have not been able to call me out on. The act of vulnerability is one of the biggest catalysts for growth and learning.

In doing so, you reveal more of yourself. Sometimes, we think we know ourselves but forget to check our blind spots. We think we can ignore them, suppress them, paint a picture and nobody will notice, but they will always find their way up. The right people will help you learn how to navigate and not feed the desire to run. Even in moments of adversity, a true friend remains. Proverbs 17:17 straight up says, " A friend loves at all times."

Chapter Eight

One day, I was praying to God, and I heard the Holy Spirit ask me, "What lie was I still holding on to?" One of them was that I was not enough. It's a lie I struggled with for a long time. He reminded me that The Word is a sword and that I needed to kill the lie, so I was brought to Psalm 139:14, which says, " ..I am fearfully and wonderfully made". Although familiar with that verse, I kept returning to the word "fearfully." I opened my Blue Letter Bible app to dig deeper. One of the definitions that stuck out to me was "to stand in awe." It was an instant light bulb moment. A fresh revelation washed over me that to be fearfully and wonderfully made meant to be made in His image and live a life of awe. That is how He created me. He created me, and that in and of itself is a big deal, but to be made with a purpose in mind, everything just started to make sense. It was like I knew who I was supposed to be from this point on. The beauty of faith is the swell of remembering how good God is to remind us of who we are. I loved Him all over again for that sweet revelation, but I would be almost 30 before the lightbulb would turn on. Until then, I was going in circles, trying to figure out

His plans, and in the dark about who I was or thought I was. There was growing that needed to take place.

At the cute age of 23, I identified as hopeful yet confused. I identified as "it is well" with not an ounce of fight in me. I identified with creating an image of myself based on the expectations of others and wondered deep down how far it would take me. Thank God for the Word of God, which says in 2 Corinthians 5:17, "Therefore if anyone is in Christ, he is a new creation. The old things have passed away. Behold, all things have become new." He would make me a new creation in Him years later. There would still be leaves to shed.

Up to this point, I had blindspots that I wanted to keep hidden, so I was okay with hiding among others. I didn't know exactly who I wanted to be or have any major plans on the horizon. There was no brand I desired. I didn't think of myself as front-facing in any way, but I knew I wanted to be good and do good, whatever that meant. Sometimes, the being and the doing take a while to meet up. I knew definitively what I didn't want. That's often easier for us to figure out than the latter. There were parts of me that I was still ashamed about, pieces of me that were not yet healed. There were still pockets of " what ifs" laced with "so and so's." Those pockets would leave me empty at times.

Overall, I was at peace, had pockets of joy, and was still pursuing God. So, what could be the problem, right? My joy had arrived, in different areas, as my name would suggest, and still it left me feeling empty. Now and then, a cloud of "higher education" would come over me, but it was nothing I wanted. I also did not know what I wanted. If I choose this moment, to be honest, the truth is that a lot of what I wanted for myself, others didn't want. Likewise, a lot of what others wanted for me I didn't want. As a result, that leaves me sitting still to avoid a high tide or swim in the waves. I was afraid of drowning, and I let time pass rather than find another way because maybe deep down, I knew who I wanted to be, but outwardly, I wasn't ready to let that part of me reveal itself. I was fearful of who I could be.

Outwardly, though, I couldn't let these thoughts manifest. I played the role of keeping it together. I was just starting to understand it and would go on to perfect it for many years until I couldn't any longer. We peel back a lot of layers as we grow into ourselves. For some of us, we grow best when we are exposed, raw, yet surrounded from the jump. Then some of us grow best hidden, exposed in secret, and yet still surrounded. I was in the latter. Through this process, even as I write, I realize that God had to show me who I was by keeping me hidden in the safety of those who knew Him and knew me. Otherwise exposed, I would be distracted.

Coming into yourself, there is so much that can play as a distraction, play on our emotions, thoughts, and weaknesses. Who are we supposed to be? Some people know right away, and others don't. Both are perfectly ok. In waiting to figure it out, we can find ourselves looking around at how things are being done and see where we fit. However, it's a weird waltz we find ourselves dancing with identity. We decide which pieces of the world we want to partner with and which pieces we don't want to acknowledge. I often wondered which areas I could compromise and how that would shape my identity. The world will say, "Only God can judge me," but when that day happens, would I be ready? If the judgment of God came on me at 23? I wasn't living in reckless abandon, but with God, the sins are all weighed the same, so as someone who gossiped endlessly, for instance, my bed was made. But thank God for grace, the grace to learn and grow and develop time after time, because that is how we find ourselves, and that is how He shows us who we are.

I would come to learn that my identity is in Christ, and as a believer, it's one thing to hear someone say it and be aware of the terminology, but it's different when it begins to burn in your heart. Understanding my identity, I was fighting battles within myself that told me I had no worth, would be alone, or needed to have a certain thing, know a person, or be at this milestone. All of that is good and well, but if we should know anything, it's that it is all temporary. It's fleeting, for we should understand the truth of Philippians 3:20, which reminds us that our citizenship is in heaven.

It is not that wanting things is wrong, but when they become an identifier, we may drift in the wrong direction. That is the beautiful thing about our identity being found in Christ. It's a sure thing that keeps us on the right path. We must know it for ourselves and remain in Him. 2 Peter 1:3 tells us, "seeing that his divine power has granted to us all things that pertain to life and godliness..." It's one thing to know scripture, but it's another to meditate and have it permeate your life.

Knowing it for myself took work, work that I was too lazy to do because it meant stripping off weights that I was comfortable carrying, although not mine to bear. There are some identifiers we hold on to that are out of our control. It is not bad, but because we are human and have our faults, we turn them into burdens and limitations. I identified as a firstborn daughter, and I identified as a child of divorced parents. Neither was within my control, yet I turned them into a stain on my identity as if they held me back from being all I was meant to be. When God knew how my life would plan out before I was formed, how dare I put a limitation on it? But we do because we are human.

We all have one thing or another that we may have subconsciously allowed to put a limitation on the truth of our identity, whether we spoke it over ourselves or through circumstances. They are just not true to who God made us. However, in maturation, we take the limits off and allow God to reveal the product of our identity through each situation. This is what I was learning. This is how I was being molded: to remove limits, to be bold, to put on my new self, to identify as He created me, to bet on myself, and to trust Him all the way. In finding my identity in Him, I began to put my faith into action, even the unseen, because I knew how He wrote my story. And, as I identified with Him, I found peace.

I have seen many people search for their identity with vigor, as if life ends at 30, so you must figure it all out before then. The truth is we should seek out our identity because the grace and mercies of

God allow us a new day to try and come closer to who we truly are, who He has made us. I like to think that ages are just a checkpoint, perhaps for milestones in the natural. But who we are can show up at any moment and at any age. We only need to be ready to walk in the fullness of our identity, which is now revealed to us. Who we are may be a surprise to us, but it is not a surprise to the Lord. If we slow down, we see that our identity has shown itself time and time again if we only give ourselves a moment to see.

Chapter Nine

Coming into myself also meant coming to understand one of my biggest personal struggles. For a long time, I was struggling to understand my purity and womanhood, my modesty and vanity. I struggled to understand the truth of what those things looked like for me according to who God said that I was.

I'm 24 now, but I don't feel like I am. I often don't think I look my age or any older age. I don't look like the girls on social media, and not that I want to, but I want a change. I want to feel older, feel grown. To say it straight up, I want to be sexy. Yet, I'm not sure how to do that. I don't think I can do that as a believer because what would that look like? I don't want to cause temptations, but I want to feel desired, and yet I don't want to be wanted by just anybody because I am desired. How do I define my womanhood? How do I come to understand I was created this way for a purpose and remember that there is a time, place, and one person with whom I can share the beauty of being a woman?

These are the circles my thoughts often spun in and kept me in one spot, not moving forward or backward, just thoughts and stillness.

Often, purity culture and modesty culture can present themselves with a list of do's and don'ts, expectations that make a person feel insecure or unsure of themselves and who they should be. In the past, the church has done little to talk about purity and help us understand why we should keep it. If anything, the church often made it seem up to the woman to keep hers and said less about it to the men. Purity may seem like an ugly word. A word that people use to control and police a woman, when that is not the case. There is a way for both a man and a woman to live purely.

In elementary school, I physically developed quicker than many other girls in my class. I wasn't yet a woman, but I was no longer a little girl. Additionally, as time went on and entering middle school, I was unintentionally exposed to different things. Through what was in the media, through friends, and other curious teens, I began to learn a thing or two about the body. Things that were not so pure. I was curious about life like many of us are, and just like that, purity became a struggle for me.

It doesn't always get better as an adult. In a day and age where you can see everyone and everything and recognize what garners more attention. How much more for a younger person? It can be a constant battle. I remember I would make excuses for what my body was feeling and say, "Biologically, this is normal; sex is normal, and desiring it is normal." However, there was an intention behind it. There is a foundation to everything that God created, even when we don't see it at the time. There were many moments where my actions and thoughts were impure, and I would forget the intention.

Sometimes, I would forget my why, "Did I want to wait?" "Was it going to be worth the wait?" "What foundation was I standing on?" "Was I considered more or less than because I waited?" I just wanted to get it over with. It felt like a dark cloud of suspense hanging over my head. Would I be the female 40-year-old virgin? Maybe a touch here and a kiss there and it would be ok, toying with compromise. And for me, part of what I felt made me a woman were the sensual and tender parts that I had to keep locked up. It wasn't the only thing, but it was a big thing.

It's one thing to do something when you are unaware and don't have the spiritual understanding or groundwork to walk on. That's different. It's straight-up ignorance to know what should be done and do the opposite. As time passed, opportunities presented themselves; hormones raged. Even the famous "biological clock" was starting to reveal itself, and I was beginning to fold. I was willing to follow ignorance over my faith. Lust and perverse thoughts are the secret sins. The sins we often try to cover up but still reveal consequences time and time again.

God did not design sex to be complicated, but we complicate it ourselves and can allow so much extra stuff in when we do it out of the confines of what He intended. My views and expectations had been tainted. Yet, He remains merciful, even though we abuse His mercy. I was looking at the idea of purity, or lack thereof, through the views of the world and did not understand what I was holding on to. I had to understand that He protected me from potential hurt. I was treating my idea as a woman as something contingent on what I gave another man when He created me outside of that person to be a fully beautiful and complete woman.

Yet of all the actions, thoughts, and desires of my flesh, I wouldn't let myself go down that hole completely, and over and over in my repentance, God picked me up till I couldn't go near it at all. I did not have to fight my flesh any longer. The thing about true repentance is also that, even if I did not wait, I wouldn't be looked at differently in His eyes. I wouldn't be less than or judged by Him because He gives a clean slate, a Tabula Rasa.

God snatched me up out of the daze of lust, perversion, shame, worldly curiosities, and sins that I tried to convince myself that I would be ok with should anything happen. I could never go all the way. I wasn't fully developed in understanding why, but I knew He was keeping me and covering me against the weeds and temporary winds trying to make me bow. He was going to keep me until the right time. It is truly the fruit of bearing discipline and self-control.

While one part of me was being pruned and purified, another part played touch and go with modesty and vanity. Figuring out how much my appearance mattered to me would be complicated. As purity was internal, it was easier to hide from the inside out without many knowing. Modesty was the opposite.

It was an image, the perception of others. It was subjective. I am reminded of a portion of the verse in 1 Samuel 16:7, often spoken out of context: "For man looks at the outward appearance, but Yahweh looks at the heart." The problem is that sometimes people use that verse as a scapegoat to look outwardly anyhow and finish off with " only God can judge me." Trust me when I say you do not want His judgment, as there will be no bias.

That verse was written in context because Samuel was looking for a king and did not see what the Lord saw in David. God would later grow David to be inwardly and outwardly one of the greatest, though misjudged in the beginning. It can be tied to modesty or reflect an image that we should not look at the outward appearances of others and place judgment. But what if, as women, out of discernment and discipline, we allowed our inner heart and outward appearances to match?

My inner heart and outward appearances, as they pertained to fashion and clothing, were not yet in sync. I knew my body for the most part and what certain clothes could highlight. I was sly. I knew how to be a tease. I was vain in that I loved how I looked and how people looked at me. I knew how to toe the line and still maintain some innocence. But what happens when you renew your mind as a believer? Suddenly, I didn't want the attention I used to get, and I felt naked in my old clothes, and these were my convictions.

I felt personal conviction and shame. Yet, I didn't run to find understanding and clarity. I wore clothes that would swallow me whole, all in the name of what I thought modesty required of me. I went from one extreme to the next. I didn't want eyes on me, so I wore what didn't draw attention. I didn't want to be drawn into the vanity of beauty and fashion. It was early in my faith walk, and I wanted to focus only on the Lord.

Give me dove's eyes because what did my style matter? And yet, being human, I was still conflicted. I know being made in His image did not mean walking around with a sac cloth and paper bag over my head, all in the name of the gospel. I could still dress in a flattering way. It isn't all vanity.

But how was I supposed to dress feminine? Did I have to get rid of all my crop tops? Would showing ankles or a collarbone have me sent away? What was the standard? Where was the balance? Where was the root? Could I be sexy and remain modest? I didn't want to "shake the table," as some say. It would be a long time before I settled into my individual style as a woman. Style would constantly evolve, not because of what was changing around me, but what was changing inside me.

I kept myself unappealing, thinking that I would be less of a distraction, but I was feeding my delusion as I began to wander from obsessing about myself to how others looked. While these are all thoughts and feelings that nobody but myself knew, I knew that I was falling into a cycle of comparison, confusion, and guilt for wanting to feel beautiful when it wasn't a sin to begin with.

Psalm 94:11 states, "Yahweh knows the thoughts of man, that they are futile." The thoughts I carried about myself were worthless and shaping me for the worst, and this was all self-inflicted. Modesty should not drive you to lose yourself. I was getting lost in my head about what I thought I should look like when, time and time again, we are reminded that it is our inner mind and renewed spirit that makes us beautiful. I knew it got bad, and I had some inner work to do when a friend of mine flat-out said, "Mide, you have body dysmorphia." A quick Google search confirmed that I was indeed struggling with my self-image. I viewed myself with a microscope. Everything felt like a flaw. Everything I wore felt like an enhancement to the flaws. I could not see my beauty in the mirror. But if I didn't begin to see myself as who He made me, if I didn't begin to walk upright and in the fullness of His love, it didn't matter what I had on; I would have a tainted image.

I had to do the inner work. If you think low of yourself and your image that it takes a toll on your way of life, I encourage you to seek a professional. I did not have a case of needing a professional, but my friend's statement required me to make a mindset shift. I had to stop speaking down on myself and comparing myself to other women. I had to recognize how much I had grown. I had to sit with myself, remove the voices from way back when, and listen to the only voice that mattered, and then I began to truly see myself. I looked in the mirror and said, " Oh baby girl, you look good today." I knew the image I wanted to reflect. And in that image, modesty wasn't what I pursued anymore. Instead, I strived to look like the daughter of a king. I had to check the posture of my heart.

As women, we are beautiful, so we should show it. We also have to give ourselves grace and love for each version of ourselves. As we get older, becoming wives, mothers, sisters, aunts, and just betters of ourselves, through celebrations and moments of grief, our bodies change with time and remain beautiful. Our different styles, shapes, and ideas are all a part of how we were uniquely created. It's not vanity to get dressed, buy a purse and wear the shoes, or follow trends. It's not vanity to want a compliment, but we shouldn't idolize and use it as a metric. Skinny jeans today, cheetah prints tomorrow, cutouts left, right, and center. Fast fashion, High fashion, How do we even keep up? We mustn't lose focus. We often get so tied up in terminology and specifics that we lose the main focus.

This was my focus; if, after I got dressed and looked in the mirror, I could call on my Father and know He was pleased, then I was fine. However, if I felt an inkling of conviction, maybe showing too much here or giving the wrong idea here, then I would change. This helped me. It allowed me to decide what modesty was for me. It dropped the curtain of vanity to see a new image of self. It also made me feel safe to realize and recognize the only voice that mattered.

By origin of definition, the word modesty means "keeping with measure." So, if we measure by the world, we are limited to thinking, growing, and fashioning ourselves to the world's standards, which are ever-changing and ever-critical, leaving us unsure even with trends around us. But if we remove the measure and lean on the Lord who made and fashioned us, the idea of how we dress and see ourselves is limitless and beautiful.

Chapter Ten

So here we are now. I did not think 24 would be that transformational age, but it was. 24 was the age of unexpected growth. I was learning a lot, developing strong roots in different areas, and starting to break through the soil. I can't say I was fully mature in any area, but I was moving in an upward direction, and the stems were starting to appear. I was learning how to walk in limitless potential even if I wasn't yet executing anything at all. I still had many questions in my heart, but not yet the boldness to act out loud, so there was still waiting being done. But I continued to listen for direction and kept my "head on a swivel," as some would say. My community, actions, and environment were allowing me to grow in maturity and, in some instances, forcing me into maturity.

No greater a time was I stretched in maturity and growth than when it came to serving in the church. Whether or not you choose to serve in church or a different capacity, at some point, it will stretch you to new limits. From a young age, I looked at serving as something your parents made you do, like joining the choir even when you can't sing. For those of us who grew up in the church, they instilled in us that we all have a part to play as the body.

However, I learned maturity is recognizing the necessity to serve and knowing how to apply that need or maybe even a new desire to grow where you are planted. We all have the potential and possibility to be called to a life of service at one point or another. As things started to come together at 24, I began to feel that burden on my heart in a new way. But whether it is for a long time or a short while, service is an integral part of our journey as believers, and many of us start that action in our local church.

I had been serving in my church for a few years now, and it had become a regular part of Sunday activities until there was a switch. I will never know how God did it. Still, He took five unique women under the leadership of two other women and literally threw us into the sea with no lifejackets on to create a baptism team and begin a duty of service that quite literally changed my perspective on how I thought one should serve and what the body of Christ needed. I didn't know it then, but being a foundational member of the team allowed me to understand sacrifice and strength no matter what.

It was 2019 when I joined the baptism team. I doubt any of us knew how it would mold us as leaders or just as people, but it did. I speak for myself when I say that as I continued on that team, my heart posture changed. Since baptisms were done once a month, we each got a month, which we led, ensuring everything ran smoothly. Of course, the first month we would work as a team would be the month of May, a month that has always simultaneously brought me joy and sadness. Of course, we would serve on the busiest Sunday, Mother's Day, and of course, I was chosen to lead that first month. I felt like a little fish swimming with sharks. I think we all did at different points. As time progressed though, we found our way through the waters, not because we knew what we were doing necessarily, but because of the community and support we found in each other. Every month was something new: short on supplies, last minute run around, weekday setups, serving multiple services, in the rain, in the snow, with the cicadas. Sometimes, everyone couldn't be around to help because we all still had to live life outside of all this. Yet somehow, this had become a part of our lives. It was bigger than how we felt.

These are the unglamorous moments they don't speak of in ministry, although Apostle Paul did have some words for us. Serving is not always easy or fun. However, it is also never about us. I had to remember that every part of serving was about God's people, and Jesus died for these people out of love. It was not a small thing. You don't want to serve out of obligation. You want to serve out of love.

My time serving was not my first time serving in my local church, but it was this moment I realized what service meant to me. Through each month that came by, whether something went wrong or something went right, my joy was in knowing someone found their way back home to God publicly. I loved the feeling. I loved speaking with folks right before and hearing what made them want to make that decision or watching people cheer them on and celebrate. I loved encouraging them in their apprehensions and then watching their faces light up, knowing they had made a bold and beautiful decision. However, down the line, that zeal got lost.

Perhaps I got tired, or maybe it became too routine, but I began to forget my why. In time, I started to resent serving. The people and ideas around me did not connect, and I was losing my why. I honestly remember saying that I felt like I was clocking in and out of work when this was something that should be celebrated.

The team had changed over the months. I had built a solid relationship with these women, so I still had my girls for life, but I was serving solo this go-round. I remember sitting down one day in observation, knowing that my heart for service had changed, affecting how I saw people and the church. And therein lay the problem. I was looking at everyone and everything except for God. Colossians 3:23-24 says, "And whatever you do, work heartily, as for the Lord, and not for men, knowing that from the Lord you will receive the reward of the inheritance; for you serve the Lord Christ." I started looking at the actions and motives of others and blaming them. I was looking at the environment in annoyance rather than serving and celebrating no matter what. In the beginning, when things were new and challenging, my attitude was, "It's not about me," and somehow, over time, I managed to make it about my emotions and my heart, what I couldn't handle, and where I needed to be. Were there issues? Of course, but that's what happens with imperfect people.

I have seen many times in serving in the church that we lose vision, not in how we should serve, but in that we should serve unto the Lord. For me, that was the case. I stopped serving. I needed to get away. I needed to reset and find God's voice again because now I was in the sea and somehow alone in it, just me. Somehow, my soil wasn't in the best shape anymore, and I was starting to wilt. I was overwatered, but not in the best way. So, I started over. I jumped ship and back into the arms of the Lord little by little. I listened for Him because I desired it, not because I was told to. I returned to the foundation of The Word and learned what it meant to serve and the expectations. I believe that is the beautiful action of service, true service, and remembering that the why always brings you back to the Lord. That, to me, is the maturation of faith, knowing to run back to Him and fixing our eyes on Him in all things.

Part Three: Mature Plant

"Remain in me, and I in you. As the branch can't bear fruit by itself unless it remains in the vine, so neither can you, unless you remain in me."

- John 15:4

A Garden in Bloom

Chapter Eleven

C an you really turn 25 without a quarter-life crisis? Yes, you can. I spent my time eating paella and sipping sangria in the beautiful town of Barcelona. I opened the age, walking through the Sagrada Familia and living out my heart's content as Galaria Garibaldi from the *Cheetah Girls*. To all the birthdays that came before and to the ones that would come after in my twenties, this was my best year ever. The lime green dress worn for my birthday dinner the night before flying out should be framed as a memory. I remember reading up on the quarter-life crisis articles and thinking how much it made sense that one would freak out because of societal, cultural, and self-imposed expectations that truly hold no ranking to the plans of God. Of course, I thought I would be married with a child and a house by this point, but where did that idea come from? On the one hand, many of us are now three years post-undergrad, maybe well into our professional careers, and yet we are also five years from 30, so there is still so much possibility. At 25, I was lucky not to feel like there was a lack in any area. I didn't have it all figured out, but I was living and living very well.

A Garden in Bloom

I looked so good that year. I was feeling myself. I was in the best shape physically, having begun to find security in my appearance. I had a strong sense of community, where I wasn't just pouring into others, but I was also being replenished. I was also full of true joy, living in the name given to me. I thoroughly enjoyed this age and all that came with it, and with good reason, because it would be a different story a year later.

In Matthew 13, Jesus teaches on the parable of the sower planting on four different types of soil: hard path, thorny, rocky, and good. I can confidently say by observation and self-awareness that at 25, I was planted on rocky soil. As the Bible similarly describes, it may have looked good because growth was happening, but life would once again show where I wasn't rooted. Life will always reveal where we are exposed. However, I was good at this point in life because I had hit all the hard points that I thought life could and would throw. From academics, unhealthy relationships, mental battles, finding my identity, grieving, watching friends grieve, to losing myself to one sin or another and coming back victorious, it was now time for me to enjoy. I was walking in the false humility that my faith had carried me through and brought me to grow but not quite bloom. At this moment though, I was growing. There was evidence that life was moving forward. This is what happens when we are rooted in rocky soil. Mark 4:5- 6 mentions the soil again: " Others fell on the rocky ground, where it had little soil, and immediately it sprang up, because it had no depth of soil. When the sun had risen, it was scorched; and because it had no root, it withered away."

As it was written in The Word, it became evident in my life. Although I was enjoying life and freely living I will admit to not being as rooted; my faith was surface. Though I was serving and present, I was operating on the contingency of what God would do for me and the things I had in place for 25 and beyond. Just because I entered this next quarter with peace didn't mean I would float through this age without expectations. I still had my plans, and I was one foot in and one foot out if it didn't all work out. Many of us tend to behave that way whether we do it intentionally or not.

I had big expectations for the next five years. I believe I had planted some seeds and shared parts of myself with others relentlessly and with the expectation that my time was now. I was entering into this new age, ready to make waves. I once heard a pastor say, "If there is no one around you benefitting from The Fruit in your life, then you have none. Fruit is meant to be consumed." He was right. However, my life did bear fruit, which I freely gave. I was living with the thought that I had shared baskets of myself for some time now, with my time, energy, finances, everything, to any and everyone, and now it was time for me to begin to enjoy myself. I realized that in the months to come, while I began to cheer many more people on and continue to show up for others just as before through milestone moments, without exception, there was a silent agreement I made with the Lord, one that said: "At this moment I'm ok, but if You don't do XYZ I can't promise how I'll be tomorrow."

Let's be real. We all have bargained, whether in our hearts or boldly out of our mouths. We have bargained as if it could change a situation. During our twenties, we are truly just trying to figure everything out, and we cast wide nets, sometimes hoping for something to stick. Or we cast nets hoping for the surprise of something new because even with everything planned out, we still aren't sure, and we're young. Things can change if we want them to. We are trying to get from one block to another, and it can be full of bargains. What do you know? Who do you know? What can you do? What do you have?

We take that same action and think we can bring it to the Lord. Or maybe you don't and never did. You have managed to go through your twenties with the security that everything you're doing is good and well, and God will handle the rest, so "I need not worry." Let me speak for myself and say I wasn't there yet, or rather, the worry came in ebbs and flows. However it came, one thing I knew was that He is simply not one to be bargained with. But those moments of truth in our hearts show that we are not as deeply rooted as we thought. Being deeply rooted means we hold on and stand firm no matter what.

The thing about having deep roots is we don't see them, but trust me when I say they are developing. In the darkness of the dirt, they are strengthening to produce fruit, potentially producing a harvest. There is a moment in your twenties when the switch flips. It wasn't 25 for me, but society can say it normally is. For some, it may be earlier, like 21 or 23. For others, it may be 28 or even 29. But a switch flips when you realize the need to be rooted and rooted well to grow. When you look around and see that what you thought was firm can be pulled up from right under you, what are you left with? How is the fruit of your life starting to look? It was at the age of 26 when I, like the rest of the world, saw the rug pulled from under me. However, it was also the moment of true maturity in more than one area.

Chapter Twelve

I f I could ignore the next few chapters like I ignored the next few years, you would understand that we have reached 2020. I have nothing to say about the events of 2020 except to thank the Lord for seeing me through, seeing all of us through. I expect that year's events to be marked in my grandchildren's history books, hopefully in truth. But outside the obvious events of the year, I found myself uneasy, and it had nothing to do with the outside world. I had just come off the high that was turning 25 and was full of hope and expectation. Suddenly, I felt like I was in a pressure cooker and didn't know what was cooking. That's the beauty of life. It can give you whiplash. It was like everything I built within myself I was beginning to lose sight of. I was quoting Jer 29:11 and could not see a single plan.

I took a job I knew I should not have taken after I walked out of the interview, but I wanted the money. The next 12 months would be manic because of it. I started a new role that I never would get the hang of. I worked with people who had me looking over my shoulder every 10 minutes. I don't recall ever seeing my manager again after the first week, and I was there for a year. Outside of work, I was losing my desire to serve in the church, and my vision was getting cloudier and cloudier. I fell into routines, old habits, and desires to create a safe space for myself. The world was losing itself right before our eyes, and we were all trying to get by. I felt myself playing tug-of-war with faith. At this point, I knew a lot about God and enough that I should not have looked at things from the world's POV, but I couldn't help myself. I kept holding on to faith but also wanted to let it go because what was the price?

Having faith can sometimes be inconvenient, but a life without God is the biggest inconvenience. The following 12 months would show that even in the inconvenience of faith, we must press on. The next 12 months after that would prove its necessity. In 2020, I was blessed. Amidst all that was happening in the world, I felt sheltered. Psalm 91 says, "A thousand may fall at your side, and ten thousand at your right hand, but it will not come near you." My eyes saw so much, but I held on to that word. This would all make sense eventually, nothing would come near me. There are moments when you have to trust God because science, medicine, and what is being shown in the media do not make sense. Social media and socioeconomic battles are rising, and you have to decide whether it's a battle you want to fight on the frontlines or elsewhere. What did fighting look like for you? That year was battle after battle, and for many people worldwide, no fight was left by year-end.

For me, I wondered if God was present, but just as quickly, I had to retract that thought because I knew I couldn't have finished the year without Him. He had a proven track record of faithfulness that I was beginning to see clearly, and I wanted to delve deeper into it. It may have been a surprise to many of us how 2020 turned out, but it was not to Him. Nothing in my life has surprised Him, and He has remained faithful while I grew to figure it out on my own. I wanted to recognize His faithfulness not just this year but in my life as a whole. To do that would mean truly surrendering everything.

I didn't think I had much to surrender. However, I also hadn't reached the point of understanding exactly what that looked like. But I knew if I wanted to break fresh soil on His faithfulness, I had to release control of my environment and expectations and give Him room. Beautiful things begin to grow when there is room. Even in a storm, a flower still grows, it still heals, and it still opens to bloom. There is some pruning done in preparation for what's to come. While in 2020, it felt like the world was getting a shakedown, I did say the following 12 months would be even worse.

Chapter Thirteen

In January 2021, I was one year down through the most stressful employment, but I made it. They wooed me with a nice snack box for the holidays, and as someone who liked snacks, I was easily impressed. The job was not my favorite by any means, but I had a 3-year plan written down to get promoted to senior level and get out of there quickly. I only had two more years to go, until I got laid off. It was so left field that I asked them if they wanted me to finish the day. Was I silly? When I was anticipating the layoff last year, they told me that I had job security, and now, suddenly, the safety net was snatched from right under me. A week into the new year, I had lost my job. A few days earlier, while the country was screaming about an insurrection, my family was faced with another health scare that paralyzed us back into 2013. Back-to-back hits within a week of a new year.

With no job in sight, I woke up on the 11th and headed to church for the first day of our annual 21-day fast. I had nothing on my schedule preventing me from going, so I began driving to church at 5:30 in the morning. I turned the radio on to stay alert. A song I had never heard came on the radio. It was called *Yahweh* by Jokia, the song that would anchor me for the next six months. I was without a job for six months. The irony of life is that you can have a good degree, multiple degrees, work experience, the works, and still, we put our careers and livelihoods in the hands of other people who can choose to keep us today or sell the company tomorrow. Nothing is a sure thing, but faith leads you to who is.

The song's chorus goes, "Lead me to still waters lead me to your alter Yahweh Yahweh, that's what I call you." For six months, I clung to the name Yahweh in the hope and faith that everything would make sense, and in time, I would see. At the beginning of the year, I remember having a dream in which I was climbing a mountain, and it would take some time for me to come down. Being unemployed was the mountain. It was new for me, not having job security. Even if you live with family, it can still be unfamiliar, now depending on other people. Yet, I cannot imagine not having the reliability of family to fall back on. Truly, it is by His grace that any of us are left with our heads on straight.

The first month or so didn't feel too bad. For one, we were still in winter, emerging from a pandemic, so there was not much to do. I applied to jobs here and there and waited. Surely, this degree I took out loans for would serve me right. As time progressed, I felt the stillness that I had looking to God to do something begin to shake. I was never a part of grind culture, but not working for so long was starting to get to me, and I could tell it was beginning to affect the people around me. I didn't know what to do or who to turn to. I had made many resume alterations and connected with those I knew, but the wall was not budging. I would remember Jer 29:11 like, "ok, God, I trust you," and I would press on and apply. Though I started worrying, I wouldn't let it shake me. But it's hard to hold on to something intangible when you can't hold on to anything tangible. Time continued to pass, and winter turned into spring. It was during this time I remembered the beauty of spring. During this time, I remembered God's assignment for me to write and use my words. I would still push it back because I needed a job. I couldn't focus on anything else. The funny thing is that when God gives you an assignment, it's the only thing your mind continues to turn back to, even when life is happening around you. We each make a decision based on what He tells us to do, either walking in obedience or going in the opposite direction.

So how did I occupy my time when I felt a nudging on one end, but the reality of my circumstances was staring me in the face? I returned to the garden. Literally and figuratively, I took up an interest in gardening and landscaping, and in those moments, I began to understand the relationship and beauty between Adam and God. We could've had it all. God walking next to us, Adam and Eve in their ancient years, and us relaxing in the garden. I sometimes wonder if it had not been Eve, would it have been someone else, perhaps Cain? Or Hagar? Were we humans not meant to be in the garden forever? I don't have the answer to that. But as I entered month four without a job in sight and the walls of my room were beginning to close in on me, I found a new way to spend time with the Lord.

A Garden in Bloom

I had no experience, but in my restlessness, I decided to do some landscaping in the front of our home. There I was, uprooting every dead bush that had been abandoned. I figured if a plant died, the roots would also be weak and easy to remove, but I was wrong. I did not realize how deep the roots went and how strong they were because some of those bushes would not budge, but neither would I. I was pulling weeds and scattering soil. I had been to Home Depot and back more than I could count. My car was collecting more dirt than it should have. My body hadn't felt this much pain since my track and field days. This would be a good time to say, keep that body together! With all I experienced, I understand when they say gardening is low-intensity exercise because my body took a beating, and not in the HIIT way. I gained a new knowledge of what it meant to be deeply rooted as I burned in the sun working on one bush for 3 hours, and it would not budge.

I can't imagine what my family thought at the time, but it gave me an outlet to know I was creating something living and beautiful. Rather than wait for an interview, I put my mind and body to work. We can sometimes look at a garden and view the flowers as beautiful, but I quickly learned that beauty was in the process. For every dead thing I pulled out, I created room in the soil for a new thing. I loved it. I loved how God could speak and show me who He is, just like He did in the beginning. The same God of yesterday, today, and forever. I loved how it reignited my faith to trust and be patient for what is beautiful. God is always trying to show us what is beautiful, but we have to make room for Him to move.

I had to learn to appreciate the silence and the waiting as much as I appreciated the voices and the noise. I realized that for me, it was in the quiet that God spoke. It was in the early morning watering sessions and the planting of the marigolds that I heard Him say to remain at peace. It was during that time that I again remembered the assignment to write. But now, I had a different end goal in mind. I saw that God was making something beautiful in all stages, not just with one flower but with a collection of varying flowers with fresh soil.

I believe that living in your twenties is a collection of moments and growing pains that allow us to come into our own. It's allowing the process to go as is and trusting the Lord to make it beautiful. It's not one defining moment, but it's from the first day of 20 to the days that follow. The changes, plans, expectations, and revelations all intertwined to define a beautiful decade in faith—a decade of growth. We trust the Lord that what was planted will produce fruit as we are rooted in Him, and it will produce fruit in season. As I watered and waited, I began to see the established work my hands had done. Landscaping was not my skill set, but in the season of not knowing what lay ahead, I got my hands dirty, and as I had moments where I would cry out to the Lord in secret, I would still go outside and marvel at the garden that was blooming ahead.

Chapter Fourteen

Owning a garden is not for the weak. It is a beautiful lifestyle to maintain if one has the chance. Waiting for something to grow, getting your hands dirty, and fighting off pests is not fun, but it's all a part of the process. I remember finally finishing the bulk of my project, and now it was time to water and wait for blooms to begin. I didn't anticipate there to be any major outside issues because I was inexperienced, and still, that didn't stop them from coming. I woke up one morning and went to check on the growth, but what I found instead tore me apart. The local neighborhood deer gang had uprooted all the hard work, all the toiling and planting. Do not be fooled. They were savages, pulling my lilies out of the ground. I was pissed off! However, I returned and replanted, but it happened again days later! I went back and planted something else. Days go by, and just when I thought I had them figured out, rabbits had their fill, and then cicadas emerged. I was ready to throw the whole garden away. I was frustrated with what was happening outside, but I forgot the resistance of plants and the power of being rooted. They may have been getting destroyed on the outside, but the ability to keep coming back was because of solid roots unseen. In the midst of all that, I had two plants that I didn't have to worry about because they were so rooted and growing beautifully despite outside forces. Despite it all and with perseverance, seeds planted were producing a gorgeous harvest, although it is possible to reap a bad harvest.

Although I don't believe we do it on purpose, it is possible to plant a seed that will not produce fruit. To operate with ill intent, impatience, worry, fear, anger, envy, weariness, varying things that could weigh on our hearts and, in turn, produce no fruit. It is possible we don't know if we've planted these seeds until they produce bad fruit or issues in our lives, and whenever that happens, we have to do root work to get rid of the problem. I would come to learn how faith can produce a harvest that nothing else can. However, the weight of faith is heavy, and nothing increases the weight of faith like waiting for something with nothing in sight. I was now in month five of unemployment, and still nothing in sight. But a job wasn't the only thing I was waiting on.

I was now 27 and not nary a prospect in sight either. My DMs were dry, the grocery store runs weren't revealing any prospects, and even the Home Depot I ran up and down in did nothing. Every rom-com I had watched and thought to be realistic was proving to be a dud. The fact that I had to find myself, find my community, find my purpose, find a job, find a man, and still keep my peace was getting ridiculous. It felt like a needle in a haystack, and I didn't know where he was. I would be lying to say it didn't bother me because it did. I wanted to be a young wife and mother, and although I wasn't old by any means, I didn't have all the time in the world either. But although dating is not always fun, it is a necessary means to an end, that end being marriage, which in turn points to another mission, but we aren't focusing on that now. The reality of my dating life thus far is that outside of, for lack of a better word the "situationship" that happened in my early twenties, I hadn't been on that many dates. Not because I didn't want to and not because men were lining up at my door and I was saying no because of some Christian girl list people think we often have. It was a dry dessert for me. However, I truly believed that God would not place the desire to be a wife and mother in my heart and not fulfill it. I was not going to compromise, and I guess what made that easy was that there was nobody to compromise with. I am not being dramatic, nobody was checking for me.

I remember going on one date and thinking, "Oh, this could be the one." But sometimes, as women, we need to simmer down. The date was a great time, laughter that showed all our teeth, the food tasted good, the conversation was better, and then I got in the car and just knew that was where it would end. It didn't work out, and although I was sad about the potential, I was also relieved since I knew that God said He would do it, but it may not be with this one. I began going on dating apps. The dating app scene is not for the faint, especially if you are traditional like me, but I had to step out of my comfort zone. I wasn't going to be found on my couch, so why not try something that was meant for such? I got overwhelmed very quickly.

I began talking to way too many people at once, and it did not feel organic to who I was. On the one hand, since it had been so long, it gave me the opportunity to remember how to talk to guys, receive interest, and revisit points that I thought were non-negotiable or negotiable. It also boosted my confidence because surely I did not walk around with a bag on my head. I tested out folks in other states, thinking it was just the DMV, but it was not working out. I took breaks and came back, remaining hopeful. However, the turning point came with my last match. I thought, surely we have finally struck something good. This guy was saying a lot of great things. He looked great and had a diverse background, but then he opened his mouth to say something that I could not understand, so I had to hang it up. If the red flag waves stronger than the green, hang it up. These apps were not for me.

Nothing is wrong with using dating apps. Be open to trying new things; just use wisdom and know when to stop. I can attest to people meeting love and finding their forever person on the apps. They do work! However, do not throw yourself at every man with a heartbeat. I wasn't in the habit of becoming a serial dater or dating for a free meal. I could get my own meals, and my time wouldn't be wasted. I deleted those apps more times than I could count, and it wasn't even about pickiness, as many would suggest. Eventually, I figured that unless the man created the app himself, God would have to do it another way. I had more peace being off of it than on it. Know yourself. The way the peace of God shows up when you walk and do things in alignment is beautiful. When everyone is going left, I have peace going right. It's nerve-wracking because you feel like the anomaly, but then you remember you don't walk alone, and that's how I saw my dating journey.

As a woman, it's a waiting game. We cannot marry ourselves and will not propose to a man. And so we wait. Are there things we can do to show interest? Sure, but ultimately, we wait. And for me, as I waited, I learned that waiting looked like loving myself all over again. It looked like healing the broken parts of me that I did not want to bring into a marriage. I know I said I wanted to get married young, but I'm sure if I got married at 24 with all the skeletons and bones in my closet, I would be on the road to divorce. The older you get, the more you don't want to date for the sake of it. It's best to move intentionally so you don't leave your heart vulnerable. So, for me, it was quiet, sometimes too quiet. As I went from one wedding to another, I couldn't help but wonder when. Always a bridesmaid, yet to be the bride. I was starting to build a collection of bridesmaids' dresses, and fear was shadowing behind me.

Thank God for friends who pull the weeds of self-doubt and fear out and water you when you're dry. Thank God for friends who water you with the truth and promises of God. A dear friend once said, "Imagine you get married in a year. Have you done everything you wanted to do while you were single?" I had never thought of it that way, and I remembered having a few conversations with women who were saying they wished they had done XYZ before getting married or before having kids. My answer was no, and that helped me to live again. It allowed me not to idolize a promise that I had faith God would fulfill. It helped me process and receive the wait as temporary, not permanent.

And so in that, I prayed and waited. And with the job, I prayed and waited. At this point, I had understood and knew who God was revealing Himself to be at every point in my life. Immaturity can be a choice when you have everything you need to grow, and I chose to lay my immature thoughts to the side and trust God. Maturation is waiting with the knowledge and peace that God will do it. It's acknowledging the wait, the bad with the good. It's seeing the growth of not falling into a self-deprecating funk but deciding to dance and praise Him in anticipation. It's not letting the devil see you sweat even when you're boiling internally. Two things are allowed to be true at the same time.

Chapter Fifteen

J ust as much as I was boiling internally with the mundane pressures of life, I was still burning on the outside, because I was still keeping busy with the garden in the hot summer sun. After all, I was now on month six of unemployment. If someone had said this would have been me last year, I wouldn't be too shaken. Half of the world was unemployed during that time. But now I was starting to lose myself. Praise be to the Lord who doesn't give us more than we can bear. Often, when you are coming down from a large mountain, you still can't see what's at the bottom. You know there is something good down there, but you are fatigued because you just spent so much energy trying to get over the mountain. You're running down to rest, yet at the same time, you don't want to fall, so you press the brakes. Many professional climbers say coming down from a mountain is actually harder than going up.

Interview after interview, possible career pivots, I didn't know when it would end. But the valley was near. His word says in Psalm 23 that He makes me lie down in green pastures. There was rest in the valley, and finally, after six months, I got a new job. My degree was officially not in vain. Faithful God heard and answered in season when my time in the garden was done for now. He sent me out.

So what's next? Because something always has to be next in one's life, right? Well, I felt it was time to move out. I wanted to move out two years prior but figured I would wait, get married, and then leave. Since that wasn't happening yet, and the nudge was getting stronger, I set out, though I loved being at home. I also had the means and support to do so and would not wait on a man. I needed to move out for myself. In a way, I had become comfortable, safe, and complacent in living because everything was at home for me. I needed to maintain the growth of the person I was becoming and who God was making me to be, and that wasn't going to happen fully surrounded. I needed to recognize my thoughts and needs and know how to act on them. I also needed to not be needed, and as a firstborn, that's a whole other book. For me, it was time.

Moving out is different for everyone because of different circumstances. Everyone has their own time, some 18, some when they marry, some 30+, and with the state of the world as it was economically, I don't blame them. Perhaps it is for mental sanity, or life just places you in a new location. Do it when you really have to, not because it's the in thing or you have the money. Even if you have the money, if you can hold on to as much of it as possible, do it. Leave when it's your time, and only you will know your time. Everyone has their own time and way of going; for me, it was 28.

When you move out, you realize you need your own faith. You can't borrow or lean on someone else's as before. As I bought kitchen items and began to look for furniture, the shock of some of these prices was not a joke. Why would a rug be in the thousands? Why did it feel like everything was in the thousands? Anyway, I knew the Holy Spirit would prune me as soon as I left. Everything in me knew this move was out of necessity for God to speak to me loudly and uninterrupted.

Everything in the garden is not always healthy. You see the beautiful flowers and leaves, and yeah, you notice a little browning on them, so you brush it away and call it a part of nature. However, what you do not realize is that by ignoring that small brown part, you allow room for it to grow slowly. Ignoring old habits or thoughts, thinking them to be fleeting until they return as part of your lifestyle.

I believe that God separates us as we grow to new heights. He identifies and pulls out things that you thought could be ignored or unimportant. He separates us, not to be alone but to be pruned. In John 15:4, Jesus says, "Remain in me, and I in you. As the branch can't bear fruit by itself unless it remains in the vine, so neither can you, unless you remain in me." In all the ways I created my home externally, I had to update my home spiritually. I pruned into beauty.

Part Four: The Flower

"Now faith is assurance of things hoped for, proof of things not seen."

- Hebrews 11:1

A Garden in Bloom

Chapter Sixteen

T here are many benefits to pruning a plant. It helps to get rid of diseases, and it allows for better aesthetics. Another important benefit is that it promotes new healthy growth. It's like they say, " out with the old and in with the new." You can't grow if the soil isn't good, the water isn't clean, and your environment doesn't change. Correction, you can, but why be a rose from concrete when you can be a rosebush in the garden?

Well, my environment took on a new name. After months of searching for a place to call home, desperately wanting a specific type of place, having my credit run through, and bidding for properties that were not mine to own, I found peace and comfort in my first apartment. I had my keys, my own address, and bills to pay now. I believe it's a surreal moment when you first get your place at any age, and without a roommate. It's like, "Whoa, this is mine; I'm really the boss," and also, if stuff hits the fan, it's essentially on me. I was giddy with joy, but also, a voice in the back of my mind knew God was getting ready to shake me up and wake me up real quick. However, for now, I enjoyed getting comfortable.

Comfort lasted for only a short time. After a few months, I was as set as I wanted to be in my space. I had a routine, I had necessities, and I had a lot of candles. What more could a girl want? And yet, the allure had begun to wear off. Now, I had nothing to distract me from the fact that I was alone in a new space. Proverbs 16:27 is often misquoted as "an idle mind is the devil's workshop" when, in reality, it says " an idle hand." My hands and mind were both idle, and the enemy had his tools ready to go. This was the beginning of the pruning process. So much of life is in the ordinary, and much of the ordinary parts of living alone, the chores, the quiet, the schedules, began to fill me with confusion. It was like I felt I should do more, decorate more, host more. I could have a space and just be, but I had to do also. My identity was taking a hard hit.

Now that I was alone, who was I without the responsibility of caring for others, without the dependency of other people? What was I supposed to be doing with my time that would draw me closer to God? I felt lost in my own home. Was I allowed to take care of myself? And what did that look like? It's one thing to know who you are with other people, but what happens when everyone leaves? When you are no longer tethered to how they perceive you.

We never stop learning ourselves. The beauty of growing is that at any age, we get to reinvent, learn, adjust, and grow into hopefully better versions of ourselves and be that version. My hope is that we become the versions that God intended for us from the very beginning, blooming into full form. I had to learn in my time alone that my identity wasn't " the firstborn," "the oldest daughter," "the friend that..," or "the go-to cousin," all these titles that we hold as a reward that can sometimes be heavy.

I was able to sit and be me in all my quirks. I began to do the things I couldn't do before and enjoy the little moments and the big moments. If I wanted to make banana bread just because, I did. I could blast music and leave a dish in the sink or walk my dog in the park mid-day just because. I was allowed to just be, in all forms and all ways. I began to walk around and learn God's voice again, clearer for myself. My identity was in the Lord, and as His daughter, I started to remember my worth. We have to be mindful to remember our worth. There is beauty in seeing a dead leaf or two to make room for more. There is beauty in dying to self and making room for God, trusting in faith that He will raise you up to live a life for Him and a life still beyond your wildest dreams. I progressed like a seedling, turning from a bud, but not without more pruning.

The thing about being in your late twenties is that even when you are doing something well for yourself, many times with no ill intention, people come in expecting more. It is imperative to know who you are and whose you are. Romans 12:2 says, " Don't be conformed to this world, but be transformed by the renewing of your mind, so that you may prove what is the good, well-pleasing, and perfect will of God." How can the Bible say that, and then I consume my thoughts with the expectations of others? Under the guise of "wanting the best for you," it can also push you to do something you're not ready for if you are not strong in your faith and standing on His promises.

During my time alone, I had to identify what others wanted for me, what I wanted for myself, and what God wanted. Did they all line up? Where was the sacrifice? What was the gain? It can be hard stepping away from the expectations of others if you have been in it for so long, but it is necessary. Know that it is ok to push back safely. Having a mind of your own is vital at this point because you truly are on your own in many ways. They kick us off our parent's health insurance at 26. We better get it together. But with less levity, the thoughts and opinions of others mustn't shape our direction too much. I had to learn to discern which voices I would take into account because, at the same time, we want to be submitted to authority, but that is not everybody.

I also had to learn that every moment of joy did not need to be monetized. I remember baking a lot during the first few months, and someone said to me, "You could start selling this," a harmless comment because I do make some good banana bread. But I believe we live in a social culture where you could sew a hole in a sweater, and suddenly, you should go into design. Some of us take compliments and walk right into even more headaches because it wasn't God's plan. If God intended for every hobby or action to be monetized, when would we rest? I had to remember that it was ok to do things for me. I didn't want to jump on any bandwagon to keep busy and not live idle. I had to be conscious not to compare myself to what I saw on the outside. Boho chic was the new trend, so should I change my whole apartment? Should I switch to Tech? OK, I have a place so I guess I should get married now? From one thing to the next is not always the best practice. When do we stop and smell the roses? In all that, I had to pause and say which of those things pointed to what God wanted me to do next.

Group thinking and comparison are weeds that can choke us out if we are not careful. They start subtly, but then we begin to compromise our peace, our joy, and ourselves. I called my home a place of peace. Literally, my Nest App for the thermostat was called "Peace." If you/it didn't bring me peace, you didn't walk through my door. I was purposefully living to make sure I had the mind of Christ and walking in His path. I had to make sure that His voice was louder and His vision was clearer than everything else. Even with this in mind, He wasn't done pruning me.

It's one thing to compare and contrast your life to others, but it's another thing to judge how others live, and God was going to straighten me right out. As much as we say good things about ourselves, we have to do the same for others and not operate on judgments and gossip. Being a woman of faith doesn't place you on the pillar to now place judgment. In Philippians 4:8, Paul says, "Finally, brothers, whatever things are true, whatever things are honorable, whatever things are just, whatever things are pure, whatever things are lovely, whatever things are of good report: if there is any virtue and if there is any praise, think about these things." Of course, this is often easier said than done, but the sooner we learn the power of our words, the better. The sooner we learn to mind our business, not in a way that we don't care, but in a manner that shows our focus not on things on earth but above, so I'm not worried about what's being said, the better. We speak the truth in love, as noted in Ephesians 4:15. We have to remember that from the beginning of creation, words spoken by God turned what was void into fruition. He didn't manifest. He spoke with the authority of who He was. And when we remember that He is the same God living in us through the Holy Spirit, we remember our words and realize that for some of us, it's best not to speak. It was words spoken by Satan that would lead to sin, so for some of us again, it may even be better not to listen.

I quickly learned the beauty of 1 Thessalonians 4:11, "and that you make it your ambition to lead a quiet life, and to do your own business, and to work with your own hands..." Many things are also about knowing when to just listen and not speak. Sometimes we talk too much. Even to ourselves, we talk too much. How can you hear God when you always want to hear your voice? Yet even with that, gossip or just words from other people that you disagree with can find their way to you, and when that happens, we guard our hearts, we have the necessary conversations, and we take control because the words spoken to us and over us also hold weight. Now that I was by myself, I could walk with that authority. I was relearning and clarifying boundaries. Nobody was going to call me and start saying anything or visit and say anything. I wasn't going to do the same. Like 1 Corinth 13:11 mentions, "I have put away childish things." It wasn't a matter of being holier than thou. It was operating in the wisdom that I had the clarity to receive from God.

All of what was happening during my time alone was necessary for me to grow. Just as much as a flower comes from a seed, so do weeds. Weeds grow where there is space. I had to take notice of the parts of me that had weeds, still insecure, still doubting, still resistant, still living a double life consciously and unconsciously. They may have been planted and laid dormant for many years but then begin to take up space. Weeds try to disrupt the foundation and shake the nutrients in the soil. But faith allows us to grow past them, gives us the capability to understand the land that we possess, and uproot them.

Chapter Seventeen

W hen you begin to bloom, the favor and mercy of God begin to show even more. I like 2 Corinth 3:18 because it says, "But we all, with unveiled face seeing the glory of the Lord as in a mirror, are transformed into the same image from glory to glory, even as from the Lord, the Spirit." It's the mercy of God, and I wish I could tell you why, but I don't have an answer. I don't know why the mercy of God continues to be evident in my life time and time again when I knowingly lack in many areas. I blur the lines between right and wrong for my conscience and then move as if I am deserving. He is merciful.

They say that your twenties are a time to make mistakes, be free, try this and that, travel, save, go broke, fall in love, because you can make it all up later in life. I say that goes for every decade, and I believe that as I've grown and will continue to grow. I look back and rejoice. I look back and smile through it all. Because I'm still here, being given a chance to bloom and allow the world to see pieces of me that show I have fallen, pieces of me that are bruised and imperfect, pieces of me that are also overflowing with joy and peace, and carry fruit that is to be shared like patience and kindness and more, as spoken of in Galatians 5:22. All pieces of me that show that God is good.

You can know that God is good, and things may still not look ok, but growth reminds you not to look circumstantially or emotionally every single time. Right when you are at the edge of a breakthrough, things can begin to look like they are falling apart. I remember running track in high school, and it was always the last 100M that felt the longest and most painful, but you had to finish and finish strong. 2023 felt like the last 100M. I could see the fruit starting to appear, yet not ripe enough to eat. 2023 was my year of faith and rest because, at this point, God would have to do what He does. After all, I felt I had nothing left to offer.

I was entering the last year of my twenties and wondered if I had done everything asked of me during this decade. Not necessarily by people, but by God. Did I walk in constant obedience? Also, did God do everything He said He would do? I believe that it's ok to ask God questions. For me, it's necessary to go to The Word in context and listen for God to speak. I still had a lot of questions. Although I looked back on the last almost ten years and saw the growth, I still knew parts of me were resistant, weary, and operating in fear.

I was closing in on ten years and still had a list of places God needed to move, relationships that needed mending, and physical bodies that needed healing around me. This year's events gave me the emotional weariness of my 19-year-old self, but with the strength in faith that comes from growing up as one who knows and trusts her God. It was as if the moment the clock struck 29, the enemy wanted to throw all he had left, and he did. But for everything he threw, I had The Word as my sword. Even when I couldn't see the tangible evidence. I held on to His promises. Promises that He wouldn't leave me. Promises that He sees me. Promises that He will hear and answer my prayers.

I believe the tears cried throughout the year re-watered the roots that were prepared to carry a bountiful harvest. They were getting ready to stand tall in all their glory. The things happening around me felt like I was coming down from a mountain and facing the valley of the shadow of death. It was spiritual warfare that I now had armor for. Turning 29 brought me back to where I had been when I turned 19. This time, I had security of self because I knew without a doubt that The Holy Spirit was in me. My faith had produced a level of maturity and fruit that said not this time. There was no more back and forth, no more maybe later. There was no room for fear and complacency. The time to pray was now. The time to act was now.

As much as I was running against time, I had to trust the author of time. As much as I wanted right now, I had to endure and be patient for some things. There is a time for warfare, prayer, and fasting. But there is also a time to wait. We have to know when to do each, as a collective being one body, but also as individuals on assignment. We have to understand what faith requires. It is coming out of ourselves, needs, wants, and trusting what's to come, as mentioned in Heb 11:1. God does not sit around and throw tests our way to see if we will pass or fail. The things we all endure are part of being brought up in a fallen world. Do we fall with it or rise with God? Faith helped me to hold on through the years.

I wouldn't let go of my faith, just like Jacob held on until he was blessed. I refused to let go, just like the woman with the issue of blood who pushed through the crowd. I refused to let go, for it was Ruth who said, "No, your God will be my God." Just like Ruth said, I wasn't going anywhere anymore. So, in all things, it was time to dance like David, pray like Hannah, hope like Job, and seek like Zacchaeus because God always showed up.

You see, God has been with me, pursuing me the whole time, so why would I run and hide or run when things aren't what I want or think they should be? Why would I dare leave when the promise is right there? It would be like the Israelites, staring at the promise and unable to reach it because of their own needs, their complaining, and their impatience. He covers me to protect me and to preserve me for the right time, right thing, right moment. He waits for us to be fully mature, fully pruned, and fully prepared. The Almighty God hears me, so I listen out so that I can hear Him too.

These are the parts of faith that are inconvenient. These are the shaky parts, but on good soil, we don't rock to and fro. We trust. Though we don't know what the days will look like, we remain in Him. Things are happening around us for other people, good things, beautiful things, but that doesn't negate the light shining on you, that doesn't drain your soil to dry. Like Psalm 1 mentions, the Lord provides us with living water, and we will bloom in season.

We have to be intentional in remembering the promises—not our hopes and dreams and five-year plans, not our vision boards and expectations. Remember the promises and have faith that He will do them. We need to build our faith like the ones they speak of in Hebrews 11 as great examples of faith. Those people are known for their exemplary faith because of their obedience. They trusted God to make it all make sense and come through.

It is easier to say you will allow God to carry you and be obedient than to put it into action. Obedience is something that I have struggled with because it means relinquishing control. But isn't that what faith is? You can't have faith without obedience. It doesn't work like that. Walking in obedience can be new and foreign, but there is peace that follows it. You don't do it once; you keep going. You die to yourself daily, trusting Him and becoming more like Him. You hold on because you know the track record of God, and it is pristine. In your twenties, more than ever, you need an anchor to remember who you are and whose you are because every moment, there is a new wave. Hebrews 6:19 says, "This hope we have as an anchor of the soul, a hope both sure and steadfast and entering into that which is within the veil."

Chapter Eighteen

The Word of God says in Psalms 121, "I will lift up my eyes to the hills. Where does my help come from?" David cries out to God as his helper, trusting Him. Yet, knowing and recognizing Him as such, where was the help I needed? As I said in the previous chapter, obedience is hard, and faith can be inconvenient to the flesh, and if that's the case, one might wonder, "Why didn't you leave?" In your twenties, you could do whatever, whoever, and whenever. Why are you holding on to your faith if it can be a battlefield? Why are you choosing faith over everything? God over everything?

Grief had consumed the heart and mind of my twenties for so long, and I chose not to carry that with me any longer. You see, one thing I have learned is that life and choices are about mindset and free will. The Lord has given us the free will to choose Him. And so I chose Him because even with things not happening as I planned and prayed, everything offered outside of Him, where my next moves and emotions were based on the environment and society, would not win. It was no longer an option for me. Nothing grieved me more than those who didn't know God or come to this realization, but we each have our cross to carry.

A Garden in Bloom

Mark 8:34-38, Jesus says that if we want to be followers, we must give up our way and take up the cross. He tells us that we have nothing if we gain the world and lose our souls. To take up the cross is no easy feat. We know this because of what Jesus went through. He suffered, so we didn't have to. He suffered so we can freely live and grow in all He has for us and live purposefully. Why be a dandelion floating by when I can take root and multiply? Mark 4 also refers to the four soils spoken of earlier, and many times, we are like those planted in rocks and thorns, quickly choked up, joy short-lived. It's part of living in a sinful world.

Yet, like Peter, we must not take our eyes off God. Trust that He will carry you through into harvest, into fruitfulness. Again, I don't say all this as if it is easy, especially when you're young. But it is necessary, and there is a reward on earth and in heaven. There is nothing you miss out on by knowing and fully trusting Him. When I think of taking my eyes off God, I remember the Prophet Anna in the book of Luke. She was adamant about waiting until Jesus was born. But she didn't look like she was waiting as she continued praising God.

Waiting for something can look like concern for others, but the sooner you cast off the worries, eyes, and voices of others, the more you can make room for God. They can worry, and you are worshipping. That's how God's peace works. That's how His joy is unfailing. That's how faith is activated. We may live in different times, but the model has not changed. The Bible is the model. Faith is the model.

120

There are moments when the garden can get messy, and the bees and other creatures seem like terrors, but they are working to help the garden bloom. Those hard, uncomfortable points, those life pressures, are normal. But then you have your mosquitoes with no agenda. Don't give them room to flourish. Don't give the enemy a chance to use your life to evangelize. Persevere and have faith. Have mustard seed faith. Have moving mountain faith.

Chapter Nineteen

I started the beginning of this book by referring to a statement that my pastor said: "Something is wrong when our lives make sense to unbelievers," and it remains true and evident. For ten years, I tried to make room in spaces I wasn't meant to fill up and remain in spaces I knew I should have left long ago. But a garden was being grown, and its beauty would be for all to see. Some may be reading right now and trying to understand how I have managed to carry peace, how I have left old habits, how I still show love and forgive and pour out joy, and just be, and how I can do all of that. Our garden, so full of imperfection, can make one wonder why I kept pursuing, watering, and pulling out weeds.

The past ten years point to God in ways that don't make sense if you don't have faith. Well, the one who called us is faithful no matter what. I have seen it active for myself and in the lives around me. I know they say your twenties are the years you find yourself and explore, but many lose hope before 25. Many don't get the chance to find even a piece of what they carry and light up the world. The past ten years have been a blessing in revelation and hope.

There comes a point where we need to go from passive-aggressive faith to aggressive faith. To write about my twenties is to tell you about God. It's not that I do not panic or have fears; trust me, I do. My whole body has a complete reaction. But I am not the same person who walked onto Howard's campus after breakfast with a plan in hand. Quite the opposite, the older I have gotten, the less I have planned, and I simply trust God in faith to move. I practically conquered my twenties with the measure that I was given to bear. Even as waves still approach, I am not lost or confused. I am rooted.

I can point to God at every moment and say He has been faithful. Never has He left me forsaken or begging for bread, just as His word says in Psalms 37. I can point to Him when I didn't know how I would graduate. I can point to Him when friends and family got sick. I can point to Him when I was without a job. I can point to Him when the enemy tried to capture my mental state of mind. I can point to Him when I had $2.36 in my account and just needed my free Papa Johns. I can point to Him when I didn't know how my loans would get paid. I can point to Him when I wanted to take a break from church. I can point to Him in my singleness. I can point to Him in my grief. I can point to Him in my areas of unforgiveness. I can point to Him when I was ready to call it quits and not save myself for marriage. I can't point to Him when I didn't know who I was or wanted to be. I can point to Him because through it all, through growing into my own, I grew more with Him and more in love with Him. Because of His mercy and because He was faithful. There was nothing off limits to God. Never was I forsaken. I may have left, but

A Garden in Bloom

I wasn't forsaken because of the free will He allows and because I am justified in Him.

It is one thing to grow, and it's another to bloom. From the beginning, we all grow at different rates and under different conditions. We move forward; at the very least, we get older. Yet, I believe blooming is personal. Not every flower that grows will bloom the same. In the same mindset, how we bloom is personal. It's partially up to us, but it's the most beautiful transformation that we often see. It opens us up. A garden is not made up of just one flower but rather a collection. What makes a garden beautiful is its range, landscape, and patient pursuit from the gardener.

Our twenties carry that range. Everyone's garden is uniquely built, some with roses, some with lilies. Maybe someone out there has a fairy garden, and another has fruit trees and herbs. But what may start as one flower, one moment, will create something beautiful. Life is the same: an individual trip through a personal perspective, with many moments coming together for a bigger purpose. Though there are many influences along the way, I pray that in all of it, heed the Voice of God in faith.

There is no age to start believing, and life does not end at thirty. A garden can only grow larger and more beautiful as you tend to it. If you are reading this in your twenties, may you continue to grow and bloom fully, tending to the garden of your life. If you are reading this before and after, faith applies to all. God applies to all, and He doesn't take away the life you truly desire. He doesn't come to age you and turn you into someone you won't like. You are in your twenties, so live out your youth. Travel the world and the cities within it and see the beauty of it. Try every possible new thing by yourself or with the ones you love. Indulge in life's simple pleasures that fill you with joy. Have full belly laughs that draw tears. Quickly forgive others and show grace as new seasons and unchartered territories arise in those relationships. Build intentional relationships that water your soil and stand the test of time.

Do not be afraid to pour out yourself when you know you are filled back up. Love your body from the inside and take good care of it first and foremost. Remember who you belong to, and don't shrink back when you remember who you are. And at the core of your being, no matter what this life throws you in your twenties, thirties, and the decades to come. Let it be known that you have faith. Commit your life to the Lord and watch Him make it beautiful. Do not delay calling Him yours and having that intimate relationship with Him.

I take nothing for granted and nothing by design, that in every moment through these years, God has cultivated my life to produce a garden so beautiful. From the seeds planted and unseen, He orchestrated my days to be full of color and beauty. Even in the storms, the fragrance of His love remained in the winds. Each moment, each person, was purposeful and fed into the roots planted. May I always be like the one who returned to give Jesus thanks. May you and I always be in full bloom. Jer 17:7-8, "Blessed is the man who trusts in Yahweh, and whose confidence is in Yahweh. For he will be as a tree planted by the waters, who spreads out its roots by the river, and will not fear when heat comes, but its leaf will be green, and will not be concerned in the year of drought."

A Garden in Bloom

Acknowledgments

I call this chapter " You will know by my fruit."

I thank God, The Vine, which allowed my life to carry such healthy fruit in perfect seasons. For each person I speak of, may they continue to bear fruit in their lives as they have blessed me and even still show an art of love towards me that comes from knowing God themselves. Everyone has a story to tell, and because of the roles that each of you played throughout the years, many of you have made it possible for me to tell one of my own.

The Lord established the work of my hands to completion. I never knew this to be part of the plan, but you knew me before I was formed and saw this in sight. No matter how many times I tried to quit and hide. Peace came when I was obedient. Thank you Lord. Thank you for trusting me to be obedient.

Thank you to my editor, Chantelle, for your sweet spirit in taking on this book. Your perspective and input helped to take it to the next level.

Charlei Charlei Charlei! The cover is stunning because of your talent, commitment, and patience down to the wire! You literally took my heart and created magic. I cannot thank you enough!

A Garden in Bloom

Mom and Dad, you have supported me through this surreal process. You prayed and allowed me to be my full self with the book and without judgment. Thank you ten times over for your blessings, love, and guidance. Thank you for raising me to be a woman of faith. Thank you for being an example of remaining faithful no matter what life throws your way.

Ayobami, Ayooluwa, and Samuel. You are three of the four chambers of my heart in human form. You three are the most incredible people on the planet, and having you all as siblings is a treasure. You championed for me, and I pray God will establish your individual gifts as you navigate your twenties and beyond. Thank you, Lulu and Bami, for being one of my first readers and for your honest feedback and major support with every random call.

Jola, Niyi, and Tolani, you already know it's a lifetime of love, and your mama is cheering us down; thank you for being a part of my story!

Sandra, Felicia, and Temi, you three were among the first readers of my book, and I THANK YOU for your patience. Trying to get this out by the deadline had me pulling my hair, but you all would not let me go bald. Thank you for your opinions and feedback. Thank you for your support and for cheering me on. Thank you for the prayers! Thank you for loving me. I hope you each know my love for you runs deep.

Sofia, a few years ago, I mentioned writing, and you told me you would be ready to read when it was time. It's time, girl! If you ever changed your number from me, I would not be upset, haha. Thank you for answering every mundane call, text, and voice note. Your people and my people did a big one with our friendship.

To my Howard University sisters, from where it all began, to the mentors, aunts, and spiritual leaders who saw a reason to speak life into me and keep my faith, I Thank you.

To everyone who watered me when I needed it throughout the years. Thank You.

"My seed is a version of the vision that has not been fruitful yet." There is still more to come from me. This book is just a seed.

As Maya Wilkes would say, "Oh, girl. I'm an authoress."

A Garden in Bloom

Author Bio

A Maryland native making her debut as an author with *A Garden in Bloom.* Ayomide brings her heart for literature and writing to life. With the purpose of inspiring and boldly encouraging faith through transparency, she hopes to continue on this path with more ahead. When she is not writing her books, she "balances the books" working in corporate America. And every other moment, she takes the chance to live out life out loud, marvel at the world, and share it with family and friends with her dog Toni close by.

www.ingramcontent.com/pod-product-compliance
Lightning Source LLC
Chambersburg PA
CBHW020400130626
46549CB00006B/2361